THE TRUTH ABOUT

FALSE
MEMORY
SYNDROME

BY JAMES G. FRIESEN, PH.D.

Huntington House Publishers

Huntington House Publishers
P.O. Box 53788
Lafayette, Louisiana 70505

Library of Congress Card Catalog Number
95-80279
ISBN 1-56384-111-8

Printed in the U.S.A.

Contents

PART II

Discussions with People Who Have Survived Extreme Abuse and Their Therapy Partners

PART III

The Road Ahead

Appendices

PART I

Basic Questions

CHAPTER 1

A Preview

Does Such a "Syndrome" Exist?

As you make your way through this book, you will meet people whose lives have been thwarted. They have been falsely accused of making up memories of abuse. Some even remember being told that no one would believe them if they ever said anything about the abuse, and that is exactly what has happened. Crimes have been perpetrated against them and no one has been brought to justice. Physical injuries and emotional scars, the legacies of those abusive acts, continue to hamper their daily lives. But, they have not lost hope.

Despite brutal treatment, these people are not consumed with revenge. They only desire to live a healthy life, and to dip as deeply as they possibly can into its sweet nectar. They want to overcome a desolate past, and prepare for a prosperous future.

You will meet Gina, who has always known her mother was imprisoned for abusing her. During treatment she has uncovered memories of abuse so extreme that multiple personality disorder resulted—it was her only means of escape. In her present life she needs to hide the diagnosis. Her career would be threatened, because false memory syndrome headlines have dominated local news. Her daughter recently asked if Gina has multiple personality disorder, and she wonders whether to tell her. What a dilemma.

You will also learn about Dora's childhood family life, which was dominated by two unbreakable rules. The first was, "Don't talk, don't think, and don't feel." The second was, "Protect Daddy." He had at least eight affairs, and the whole family was needed to enforce the rules. "Don't talk about Daddy's infidelity, don't think about what it has done to Mommy, and don't feel betrayed by him." In her adult life, Dora remembered that he sexualized her, and the family rules kicked in furiously. She has received a clear message from everybody in the family, except Daddy, that she is not supposed to talk about the incest, that they do not want to think about it, and that they will try to not feel anything about it. She is invited to hang out with them, and act as if nothing happened. They all believe Daddy needs to be protected from Dora, and he is, therefore, forbidden from talking to her about the false charges. They know he sexualized others, but they do not want to think about the possibility of incest. They say her memories must be false, her therapist must not be up-to-date about false memories, and Dora's church family must be trying to take her away from them. What is Dora to do?

And, you will meet Chloe's family, which has always been a treasured resource to her. After they heard she was diagnosed with multiple personality disorder, they soundly confronted her. In the middle of the most difficult stages of therapy, she found herself spending her therapy time trying to deal with them, instead of pushing ahead with her own issues. Can she hold her head up while false memory accusations come from those she loves?

There will also be Anna, Gloria, Laura, and Alexi. Each has encountered extreme abuse, but survived. Each has been near death, but relishes life. Each has a biography polka-dotted with pain, but each still looks forward to a time when life will be far better.

What can we say to all these people about false memory syndrome? They all deserve truthful answers, the clients and their families alike. I have been looking for an opportunity to get some answers myself. The false memory syndrome movement has seemed massive and forceful, and I had not thought of responding to it until I arrived at a seminar last summer, where I was presented with a unique chance to get the truth about false memory syndrome.

The Seminar

It was Saturday, 4 June 1994, and I was sitting near the middle of an auditorium filled with psychologists and other therapists, waiting for the high-tech video conference to begin.

About two thousand of us were gathered in twenty-one cities across the country, waiting to see the live satellite transmission of a continuing education seminar. The topic of the seminar was the recent revision of the *Diagnostic and Statistical Manual of Mental Disorders: Fourth Edition (DSM-IV)*, the book which catalogs and explains psychological conditions. Therapists were eager to learn about the wide-ranging changes introduced since the last edition of the *DSM*, ten years earlier.

The video conference had been set up taking time zones into account, so that all locations would pick up the transmission simultaneously, which made live questions and answers possible at each location by telephone. It was a display of state-of-the-art technology. The giant screen brought us together as though we were one huge seminar, without requiring us to be in Washington, D.C., where the simulcast originated.

The American Psychological Association produced the program, and their five hand-picked experts were ready to go. As the transmission began, it was explained that the *DSM-IV* had been more exhaustively researched than previous *DSM* editions. Every psychological condition listed had been subjected to rigorous field studies. Researchers were able to verify, on the basis of behaviors and symptoms, just what each condition looks like, how to diagnose it, and how to clarify—precisely—how each condition is found to be different from others. These five experts had covered everything available on all topics. They had read review papers, journal articles, and books, and were familiar with the best and the latest scientific studies.

We were told the program would be divided into four sections. Each would include a presentation by a panel member, followed by phoned-in questions. During presentations we could write out questions and pass them to the aisle so they could be reviewed by psychologists at each location, who would determine which questions would be phoned in.

I paged through the outline which was handed to me as I walked in, and noticed that my specialty area had only one noteworthy change—the name. Multiple personality disorder would now be called dissociative identity disorder. The symptoms which define the syndrome had not changed since the previous *DSM:* (1) The presence of two or more distinct personality states; (2) at least two of the identities or personality states recurrently take control of the person's behavior; (3) inability to recall important personal information that is too extensive to be explained by ordinary forgetfulness; (4) the disturbance is not due to direct physiological effects of a substance or a general medical condition (*DSM-IV*, page 487).

When the panel came to this section, they explained that the new term describes the condition more accurately than multiple personality disorder. The distinctive feature of this syndrome is dissociation, a defense mechanism which disrupts a person's identity, so the new term is dissociative identity disorder. I believe it is a good, descriptive label. As I previewed the outline of that section, I noticed that the difference between dissociated and repressed memories was not discussed, nor was the now-popular term, false memory syndrome.

I live in California, where things sometimes seem different than in other places, but I was pretty sure these experts had heard what we had heard about the controversy surrounding dissociation and "false memories." The press has devoted a lot of space to this issue out here.[1] In one recent court case a therapist was found guilty of negligently reinforcing false memories in her client, who claims there is nothing false about her memories. The father of the client won a large monetary settlement, and psychology was thoroughly discredited. The woman's memories tell her that her father sexualized her. He maintains that he did no such thing, that he loves his daughter, and that she would not accuse him unless somebody had misled her. He deduced it must be the therapist, so he sued the therapist and won.

Shivers spread through the ranks of therapists when the court decision was announced. Any of us could have been the target of that lawsuit. If a person comes into my office and says she has been abused, can I be accused of creating her story? That is the precedent set by this case. Anyone can be accused.

But, other court cases have set precedents which are more friendly to people with recovered memories. One woman remembered that her father had killed a friend of hers when she was young. She reported to the police the events she remembered, after they surfaced in her adult life, and the father was found guilty. The memories were clear enough to verify specifics.[2] Detective work found her memory to be consistent with historical events. (A new trial has been set, due to technical problems with some of the testimony, so the legal precedents set by this case may not stand.) This is just one of many documented cases which suggest that dissociated memories of abuse can be accurate. For other cases which support this, see appendix A.

As an author and a lecturer on multiple personality, I have been offered spots on talk shows to join the debate about false memories, but I have not been eager to get into the media ring. Talk shows exist to generate ratings. They are not looking for thoughtful discussion—they are looking for excitement, which keeps ratings high. Ratings mean money. Perhaps the talk show hosts believe I might add some excitement.

The gambit usually goes like this: A talk show host gets me on the phone. "Dr. Friesen! Boy, I am sure glad to talk to an authority like you. Wouldn't you like to be on my show? Wouldn't you like to let people know about your books?"

I don't take the gambit. "Thank you for being so complimentary. I know your talk show is big, and thanks for offering to let me explain what I have learned. However, if there will be people on the show who say my books are hooey, because repressed memories are inaccurate, I will pass. I don't debate. I educate. If you choose me as a guest, believe me, I will give you a lot of good information. I may even be able to bring some clients with me, who would talk about their experiences. I could use an overhead projector to illustrate how memories are stored and how multiple personalities work together. We would be able to give you a memorable show, even without a debate."

Customarily, I get a "Thanks anyway," or an "I'll get back to you," but no one has gotten back to me yet. Talk shows are not interested in finding the truth about this troubling topic. If the audience may be left feeling profoundly disturbed, talk shows are not about to carry a topic. Media people need to keep their jobs and continue to make dollars. They promote entertainment, not education. It is a matter of supply and demand. The public wants to be entertained, which is the job of talk shows. Education is supposed to come from scientists and teachers.

News is supposed to come from reporters. But, the way news organizations operate these days, there is little difference between news and entertainment. A major tragedy can be reported on the TV evening news, and we hear about it from smiling faces who, in the next breath, say we can expect wonderful weather tomorrow. The listener's attention has been drawn away from the upsetting aspects of things which happen to real people. Next, we hear a movie critic's review of a horror movie. Bloody scenes appear, and the news takes on an air of fantasy. "What is the news tonight?" we may ask the listener. "Some unusual tragedies, but they don't affect me. The sun will be out tomorrow. I know how the world is, and I expect a good night's sleep." People are getting a fantasy picture of the world. The evening news is not dedicated to pursuing the truth if that leads their audience to insomnia. The free press has been gobbled up by free enterprise. We should not expect entertainers to be reporters.

The Question Is Raised

As the video conference progressed, I became concerned because the panel was not talking about dissociated memories. I knew it would be very helpful for these experts to tell us whatever they had found about the false memory syndrome controversy. A lot of people need to know, because their only source of information to date has been the news.

The panel was systematically going through the outline, topic after topic, and I kept thinking, "We have a red-hot issue and a panel which knows everything there is to know about psychology, but no one is bringing up false memories. Someone has to ask for their comments." I wrote out a question and passed it to the aisle. Momentarily, a staff person got my attention, I was ushered to the front of the auditorium, and handed a phone. I was told what to expect on my end of the telephone, and a man on the line asked my name and how to spell it. I told him my question, and was put on hold.

The panel was already answering questions from around the country. My vantage point was near the front of the auditorium, looking up from one side of the screen. I was alone in a dimly lit corner, with a phone pressed against my ear, trying to watch the screen, large and distorted from that angle. Thinking about how I would phrase my question, I tried to ignore the 250 therapists sitting behind me.

The moderator would announce the city from which each question was coming and give the caller's name as it was being printed in large letters on the bottom of the screen. The telephone was patched, live, into the sound system. Nothing was edited or rehearsed. The questions and answers were ad lib.

I was rather surprised that I was still calm. Everything seemed just matter of fact. "Okay," I thought to myself, "somebody needs to ask the question about false memories. Fine. I am willing to do it. People need to know. It's not right for this panel to pass up a chance to share what they know." I believed it was meant to be.

As the minutes passed by, it seemed I would not have a chance to ask my question. Just before the end of the time allotted for questions, my phone line came alive and I was told I would be next. Now I was getting anxious. I could imagine stammering, blurting out incomplete sentences, or getting off-track from what I wanted to ask. My focus narrowed. My name was announced as it was being typed onto the giant screen. It was too late to back out. I would be on the program in a few seconds. "Okay, Lord, here goes," I prayed.

"One issue that has gained the public's attention in recent months," I began, "has been 'false memory syndrome.' Are there any studies which list the symptoms of such a syndrome, or is there any research which shows how false memory syndrome is different from other syndromes?" I relaxed.

The panel members were larger than life up on the screen. Glancing back and forth, not certain which of them would answer first, everything went silent in the auditorium. Therapists all over the country knew that a lot was riding on this answer. The real question behind my stated question was this: "Can our profession still call itself scientific, or are the critics right when they say peoples' minds are so unreliable we cannot trust what they tell us?"

The Answer Is "No"

Three of the panelists stated they had read nothing scientific about false memory syndrome, and they were aware of no studies. They also said the term has only been around for a few months, and specified it is not a condition listed in the *DSM-IV*. They were cautious, but professional. They could say nothing about it. Their silence was very loud.

I thought that would be their answer, but it was profoundly reassuring for me to hear them come to that position. The field of psychology says false memory syndrome is not a syndrome until research documents it. There is no study which lists the symptoms, there are no field studies which document the alleged syndrome's behaviors, and there is no known way to distinguish it from other syndromes.

Two thousand therapists around the country heard what these experts said. The real question had been answered: Psychology still maintains that peoples' minds are considered reliable. We can keep our jobs as psychologists. Those who have assailed our profession because of the false memory controversy have absolutely no scientific data on which to base their cases. As Mark Twain might have put it, the rumor that psychology is dead has been greatly exaggerated. On the way back to my seat, one psychologist who is a friend of mine said to me, "No such thing! That's that."

The premise of this chapter and of this book is that the position taken by the panelists is correct. The number of studies which have subjected false memory syndrome to scientific inquiry is zero. There is nothing scientific about it. There is nothing which defines it. There is no list of symptoms which describes it, nor is there anything which helps us distinguish it from other syndromes. No studies. No such thing. That's that. We do not have to debate about something that does not exist. Until such a syndrome is identified, there is no need to even begin a debate.

But, unfortunately, that does not stop talk shows, magazines, and newspapers from drumming up interest in false memory syndrome. It boggles the mind— lots of mileage, but no fuel. There has been high-profile, public debate about something which has not even been defined. People seem to get caught up in the debate, but lose sight of real people who say they have been abused and need help.

I am concerned the debate itself is getting all the attention, and not the people. Despite the controversy, we need to take a closer look at things through their eyes. The problem is not the debate about false memory syndrome. The problem is getting help to people who have been abused.

The Problem

Yesterday, a client became visibly upset as she told me about the plight of a four-year-old boy who was visiting at her house. He asked her to come with him to the bathroom because he does not like "ca ca." No problem. She has children too, and knows that toilet training is not always easy at his age.

"You don't like the smell?" she asked.

"I hate it when they make me eat ca ca."

She knows that is often a part of ritual abuse so she began to wonder if his troubles resulted from ritual abuse. His behavior is often out of control and his sleep is frequently interrupted by nightmares. She asked him the obvious question: Who made him eat ca ca?

His behavior changed dramatically then and he suddenly became silent. She had seen that change in him before, but had not noticed what caused it. Evidently, he has crystal clear memories of abuse, at times, but when asked to talk about it, he goes blank.

When she saw his reaction to her question, my client decided to talk things over with the boy's mother. The mother said she and her son had been abducted by cult perpetrators, and were forced to take part in rituals. "That was two years ago," she said. "I didn't think he remembered it."

That kind of experience is indelibly printed on a person's mind, no matter what their age. People do not forget extreme abuse—they just cope with it as well as they can. The mother says his nightmares have been worsening lately, as has his behavior. He may be consciously aware of the abuse only part of the time, but it appears to be a disturbing unconscious force which has been increasing in recent weeks. Children are not equipped to cope with extreme abuse, and their behaviors and dreams are often driven by what they remember.

"Did you report it to the police?" my client asked.

"Yes," the mother replied. "A detective came out and investigated, but since there was no firm evidence of ritual abuse, he did not make a written report."

As she was relating this story to me, my client added there were some other unexplainable things in the story. Maybe the detective did not believe her. However, my client knows the woman well, and believes the abduction story is true. It is certainly consistent with what she observed in the child. He has become very difficult to live with, and the whole family is seriously stressed. He needs professional help, but the family lacks funds to put him in therapy. Without a police report, they do not qualify for assistance.

So what is the mother to do? She needs help and so does the child, but resources are unavailable. The detective's report would have made a big difference. That is part of the problem. I have been testifying in public hearings and speaking openly about ritual abuse for more than six years, and have found the mother's experience to be common. Perhaps authorities hope this issue will go away, so they do nothing. A report of the U.S. Advisory Board of Child Abuse and Neglect, dated April 1995, put it this way: "There is a broad-based ignorance of the extent of child maltreatment which is caused in part by incomplete data collection, inconsistent handling and tracking of cases, and little accountability among the law enforcement, medical, and child protection agencies."[3]

I find it astounding that the detective did not make a report. Perhaps he had heard something about false memories, and, sensing the controversy, left it alone. Perhaps he hoped someone else would make the report and face the controversy for him. He is not the only one who is leaving this alone. Many people who say they were abused find our society does not get involved. Sometimes I wonder how many such incidents go unnoticed, and I have to ask myself, "What kind of a society turns a deaf ear to suffering children?"

Today, a client brought me a report recently published in *The Chronicle of Higher Education* (23 November 1994, p. A6), which summarizes a study concerning ritual abuse. The client, Gloria, has vivid memories of ritual abuse as a child, knows it really happens, and sees denial in the report. It is a discouraging reminder of the many times her history of abuse has been met with denial. She is weary of defending herself when she tells people some of the things which happened to her. They ask if maybe her memories could be false. It breaks her heart. It breaks her husband's heart.[4]

The way the journal's summary reads, the editors appear to have joined those who want this problem to go away. In a section called "Footnotes," the study concerning ritual abuse is treated like nothing more than a footnote. It is deemed important enough for only three paragraphs, which include nothing about how the study was carried out. The study's title is even missing, so the reader cannot examine the study further, and is asked to accept the editor's summary as sufficient. Here is the report:

> Researchers at the University of California at Davis and the University of Illinois at Chicago recently reported results from a large survey of clinicians and law enforcement personnel suggesting that there is little evidence to show that satanic cults are practicing ritual sexual abuse of children.

Claims of satanic ritual abuse against children
have been prominent in the debate over recovered memory; a particularly bizarre case in
Washington State gained national notoriety. But
the federally supported study turned up no proof
of organized ritualistic sexual abuse of children
by members of satanic cults.

The survey did point to "the possibility of some
acts of abuse that might qualify as ritualistic,"
[according to one of the investigators] but nothing that could be attributed to a large-scale,
organized cult.

The summary implies ritual abuse is a mirage,
even though a few cases may qualify. It is shaped to
convey a popular spin: The public is gently assured
there is nothing to worry about, there is no need to get
involved, and there is no need to listen to people who
report ritual abuse.

Perhaps the public is also being asked to not think.
What evidence do they expect to find of any large-
scale, organized cult? A manual on how to carry out
acts of abuse? A nationwide computer printout listing
criminal cult leaders and their phone numbers? Written guidelines for covering up abuse more effectively?
Please, federal officials, do not waste my money on
research headed nowhere! Such acts are obviously
illegal, so they will not be documented by perpetrators. There will be no paper trail.

The people I work with are not even interested in
evidence about a large-scale, organized cult. Therapists, mothers, and husbands of victims are asking for
nothing more than support for people who have been
abused. If only ten people have suffered "some acts
of abuse that might qualify as ritualistic," will this study
encourage friends to take the victims seriously and
get them some help? I think not.

Perhaps the detective who talked with the young boy's mother had just read an article like the one above, and decided not to make a report. Law enforcement personnel will not find any evidence of ritual abuse if they do not log this kind of incident—there will be nothing for researchers to find. They can truthfully say no evidence was found, but the real truth is, no evidence was collected.

The problem is more elaborate than just finding incident rates for extreme abuse, or looking for evidence of cover-up. Nor are false memories the problem. The problem is that too many people in our country have been abused. Estimates generally run from 20 percent to 35 percent, and abuse seems to be increasing at an alarming rate. The April 1995 edition of the American Psychological Association newsletter, *The APA Monitor*, indicates current trends: A headline on page thirty-four reads, "Reported cases of child abuse and neglect are up 300 percent—a national tragedy that cries out for psychology's attention." That article quotes findings from the National Institute of Mental Health's ongoing research:

> Despite the debate over false memories of child sexual abuse, the actual reported incidence of such abuse in this country is enormous. Such cases have increased 300 percent in the last fifteen years, to about 150,000 incidents per year. Newest research in the area shows that:
>
> • Girls are four times more likely than boys to be sexually abused. But there is mounting evidence that male sexual abuse is more common than previously thought.
>
> • Young children who are sexually abused experience more stomachaches, headaches, bedwetting, inappropriate sexual behavior, anxiety, withdrawal, and developmental delays.

• Problems in middle childhood include somatic symptoms, early sexual activity, *dissociation* [emphasis added], poor school performance, [and] attention deficit disorder.

• Sexually abused teenagers are more likely to be delinquent, sexually active, and suicidal.

• Children who are sexually penetrated, sexually abused at an earlier age, or by a father or father figure fare worse emotionally and behaviorally than others.

The long-term effects of sexual abuse are highlighted by the front page headline of the same newsletter: "New threat associated with child abuse." The disturbing picture being uncovered by researchers indicates abused children face "insidious hardships" beyond the problems in school and problems with peers, which are found in other studies. It was found that abuse survivors also exhibit increased hormonal levels, and may reach puberty sooner.[5] We cannot ignore this research. Let us get help to the 150,000 reported abuse cases which lead children to problems in behavior, sexuality, anxiety, attention deficit, delinquency, suicide, dissociative disorders, and to premature puberty. Their symptoms will not improve without intervention by us. The medical and psychological costs will have to be paid. Either we decide we are going to restore these people, or the cost will be paid by them, as they live with continuing difficulties.

It seems when studies come up with high rates of abuse, people can accept that they may be true, at least on paper. But, who are the victims and who are the perpetrators? Friends or acquaintances, somebody we know, or maybe members of our family? They are somebody's friends and family. We usually do not like to think about that. Our society has yet to face what those numbers mean: We are living with forty to eighty million people who have been abused, and we are living with their abusers.

In summary, we have found that the problem has quite a few facets:

—Too many people apparently hope abuse issues will be solved by others.

—Victims' lives are seriously interfered with by abuse, by the lack of available help, and by having their accounts minimized by the authorities who should be protecting them.

—Articles which categorically label abuse memories "false" profoundly minimize the pain of those who have been abused. The "false memory" label tells victims to stay quiet. If they say anything at all, people could get upset, so they are blamed if they even talk about what happened.

The problem gets even more complicated when we look for evidence that will stand up in court. As Dr. E. James Wilder put it, "Law enforcement does not investigate crimes that they do not believe exist, prosecutors do not prosecute crimes that they do not believe the jury will believe were committed and the jury will not believe in crimes that they have not heard of before."[6] Education about memory recall and about abuse is urgently needed. The criminal justice system needs to be informed by therapists and by victims.

Research will not help us understand the problem. It does not get to the very personal, hard-to-talk-about issues that surround victims of abuse and their families. It takes time for people to open up about those issues, and research is, frankly, not suited to the task. This book answers questions concerning recovered abuse memories from a viewpoint which includes those personal issues. I have spent thousands of hours with victims and their families, and they have helped me see the problem through their eyes.

The problem is not going to go away. The four-year-old boy and many others like him will still get abused, despite our best efforts at prevention. But, I hope this book will promote understanding, equip people to help victims more effectively, stop the quarreling about people's memories, and explain how therapy gets to the truth about memories.

Having discovered already that there is no such thing as false memory syndrome, the next chapter explains some critical things about memory recall, which lead to the conclusion that there is no such thing as a false memory. Memories come from somewhere. Throughout this book, in fact, distinctions will be drawn between true memories and things such as lies or fantasies, to which the term *false memory* is mistakenly applied.

CHAPTER 2:

At the very end of her therapy session, a client asked if I was at work on another book. I

Can a Memory Be "False"?

said yes, and mentioned the title. A surprised look appeared on her face. "You mean there is no such thing as a false memory?"

My answer went something like this: Those two words do not belong together. They contradict one another—if something is false it cannot be a memory. People mistakenly think memories are an "either - or" thing—true or false. There is an element of distortion in memories, but if something is a memory there must be truth in it, and that keeps getting left out of debates about false memories. If there is some distortion on the surface of a memory, we do not just throw it out. There is still something true in it. Memories always come from somewhere. If minds produce fantasies on the spot, that is not a memory. That is a pseudomemory, which looks nothing like a memory. I help clients reduce distortions, and find what is accurate within a memory.

My client looked puzzled. She is not a person who has had traumatic memories emerge during her time in therapy. "I'll just have to read the book," she said.

That is the kind of puzzlement I often see when memory retrieval is discussed. People become perplexed. They may think I am suggesting that everyone uses dissociation, and they could have an unknown memory lurking in a corner of their brain. That gets them onto the wrong track. Not everyone uses dissociation. Not everyone recovers painful memories.

People could use some help understanding the basics about how memories emerge. The uncovering process is not easy and may take a long time. Often, the first sign of an emerging memory is the feeling that comes with it, a feeling which seems to come out of nowhere. The person senses something is terribly wrong, and seeks a therapist to get some help with the new feelings. It is not surprising that memories emerge in a therapist's office—their emergence is why therapy was sought in the first place. But, most people have not had overwhelming childhood traumas, do not use dissociation, and will not sense unknown feelings pushing into their mind.

How Is a "Repressed" Memory Different from a "Dissociated" Memory?

Repression and dissociation are mechanisms the mind uses to block painful experiences; both mean to forget. In repression, the forgetting happens gradually. In dissociation, it happens right away. Understanding how traumas are forgotten prepares us to help those whose childhood memories reemerge in adult life. They need to know that their mind is not playing tricks on them, and they are relieved to know their flashbacks do not indicate psychosis. The truth is, they are recovering from childhood abuse.

One client asked me how I can tell if her memories are true. I said she is the one who can tell: If her behavior is similar to those of other people who have been abused, and if her emerging memories indicate abuse situations, there is probably some truth to the memories. Dissociators display particular behaviors— sudden mood shifts, denial of actions observed by others, and forgetfulness, despite high intelligence.

Memories of abuse seep into daily life. Sometimes there is a powerful reliving of the original event—a flashback.[1] For more detailed information on indicators of dissociation, see appendix B.

But, the behaviors which make life difficult may be overlooked because dissociators are people whose qualities are endearing most of the time.[2] The popular misconceptions about multiple personality lead the public to expect it is easy to spot. People generally do not imagine anyone they know may be "a multiple." Nonetheless, if dissociative patterns are present, we can expect something bad has been blocked from memory.[3]

Traumatic memory retrieval needs to be understood in the context of the childhood abuse that preceded it. Most people do not know what it is like to have shocking childhood memories intrude into their conscious life, because they were not traumatized. Their mind has not needed to use the mechanisms set up to cope with traumas. To approach this correctly, people must accept that minds work distinctively under trauma conditions. The process of memory retrieval is easier to understand if we view dissociation and repression as ways the mind protects itself from the effects of traumas.

Media reports keep mentioning that repressed memories are not to be trusted. I do not hear the reports adding that if a person uses repression, they must have been through a painful experience. If repression is used, we need to state without a doubt, that something bad has happened. We cannot keep a scientific outlook if we overlook the fact that repression means something. Too often, when the word *repression* comes up, some folks throw up their hands and say, "Well, nothing can be known for sure about the memory, so let's close the case." It would be more honest to open the case back up. Even if we do not know exactly what it was, we have to conclude something painful happened.

Repression is an active process. When material enters the mind through the customary pathway, it gets recorded in the conscious mind. Despite the accuracy of the recording, it is subject to interpretation and reinterpretation over a period of time, so that it will fit in better with the rest of the person's life. Within a few months or years, it can be modified enough so that it becomes an acceptable part of the person's inner autobiography, and the original event becomes hard to remember accurately. Minds are compelled to create sense out of everything that happens, and developing an internal story aids the process a lot. When material is too painful, repression modifies things to fit into the person's internal history. In most cases of repression I see in therapy, the events have been modified so much they have been almost completely forgotten. This is sometimes called "looking at the world through rose-colored glasses." Minds use repression to keep the world looking as rose-colored as possible so the person's inner life history can be as acceptable as possible.

This is a very important aspect of understanding the way memories become distorted. They are always shaped so they seem less awful than they actually were. If a memory is considered false, we would expect it to err in the direction of making it more acceptable. Minds do not use distortion to produce a memory which is more weird, gruesome, traumatic, and unbelievable than the original event. The people who argue that "repressed memories" means "memories which are overblown by a person's imagination," do not know how repression works. Repression helps minds make things seem better than they were, not worse. It is hard to believe peoples' minds would convince them that exaggerated, horrific tales are true—

"false memories." If a memory were distorted by re-pression, we would expect it to be distorted in the direction of not as bad as the original event.

An Example of Repression

A Vietnam veteran sought me for help with his marriage. Immediately following the war, Joe dropped out of his circle of friends, and led a mostly solitary life. In the next few years, he devoted himself to a profession, married, and became overinvolved with acquiring things, to the point where he was no longer in touch with his feelings. The combat in Vietnam hardly entered his mind anymore.

He was having great difficulty relating to his wife on a feeling level. He more readily related to her in the role of creating a safe living environment for her and the family. She wanted to see their relationship get to deeper feelings, but sensed he could not get below superficial feelings.

We started looking at his feeling history, and pain-fully opened up the chapter that took place in Viet-nam. We found death, destruction, and fear. Memo-ries reawakened of crawling silently along the jungle floor, being put into many scenes of terror, and plac-ing himself in harm's way in a robotlike fashion. Com-panions were killed. He was a leader, out in front, facing the enemy, keeping in mind that when he got back to the base, drugs would temporarily relieve his inner turmoil. Following his discharge from the army, he kept busy making a living, while repression was working to create harmony between his Vietnam feel-ings and the rest of his life.

I was asking him to go back twenty-three years and let those feelings come up, so they could get the attention they should have gotten in 1970. As he be-gan to open up about his past, he gradually recalled what had happened. Repression showed up in this way: Bitterness and rage about Vietnam had given way to resignation that war is necessary. A new feeling—apathy—began to cover his huge load of bitterness, and the apathy resulted in periodic depression. But, now he was beginning to remember things long forgotten, along with the original feelings. Therapy was peeling off the apathy and taking a look at the bitterness and anger underneath.

As Joe and I made our way back into the Vietnam chapter of his life, at first we got vague images of the jungle, and then came the painful feelings which accompanied those images. We got his shock in reaction to companions being killed. We got increasing urges to find drugs to relieve the feelings. We got internal conflicts about having to face death daily, and we got rage upon his return to the United States, because he was being scorned by a condemning public.

Joe did not want to remember any of this, but it gradually came back to him. Repression had actively hidden the worst memories and the strongest feelings, but when they came back, he could not ignore them. His Vietnam experiences were now with him day and night. He could not deny them, and he could not stop thinking about them.

Therapy was reopening his feelings, and the repression-related distortions were being peeled away. Formerly repressed feelings gradually became more available to him, and the details of the memories became clearer. Preoccupation with work had kept him busy, while repression was allowing Joe to view the Vietnam chapter of his life through rose-colored glasses. As repression was eroded, he became able to talk with less distortion about specific events and feelings from Vietnam. It was not easy for him to integrate the truth about his Vietnam days, but once the material came back to him, it was always present.

Those memories did not come into and go out of his mind, but were more like a heavy load he could not shed.

As therapy moved into the phase where feelings should start reaching closure, Joe did not work as hard at eroding the repression as he did at keeping busy with his career. He dropped out of therapy at about the time his wife left him. His repression was pretty strongly in place. The deeper feelings were intense. The last time I heard from him, he was not wanting to peel off any more repression. It is not easy to take repression away, and live with the feelings underneath. Therapy for dissociators is also difficult, but the dissociative mechanism lends itself to more adaptive living when extreme feelings emerge.

Whenever I discover that dissociation is used by a new client, I take it as a "good news—bad news" situation. The good news is, this person is equipped to use the most effective defense mechanism. *Associate* means *connect*, and *dissociate* means *disconnect*. When a person dissociates, it means they have dealt with some terrifying material very well. They completely disconnected from it as though it never happened—a very effective way to deal with trauma. For example, a child can go to school remembering nothing about incest from the night before. But, the bad news about dissociation is, its presence means the person has been through some traumatic experiences in early life.

Dissociation is different from repression in these ways: Dissociated events tend to come back suddenly rather than gradually, with very little distortion, with lots of details, and there is often a sense that "this didn't happen to me." When the original event is shocking, entry into the mind via the usual pathway is circumvented. The incoming data are detoured right away, and remain set apart from everything else. The newly dissociated material has no point of contact with other information in the mind. Dissociation is involuntary—it just happens without thinking. A person does not choose to dissociate an event. Rather, the mind just reacts to the pain instantaneously, without giving the person a chance to react in any other way. The brain senses that the incoming material is overwhelming.[4]

The dissociated material is then recorded somewhere else. The experience from the painful event remains untouched by any other part of the mind. When such a dissociated event is reassociated, a flashback can occur. The recorded event replays, complete with images, feelings, and bodily sensations. Because it had been recorded in an isolated brain center, it can return to its disconnected status again. So, for a period of time, the memory goes into and back out of awareness. Therapy usually strengthens the connection between the dissociated part and the rest of the mind, so the material gradually becomes more and more available.

Whatever the person experiences is recorded precisely. If there are mistaken perceptions, or if the event includes deliberate attempts to mislead the victim, that gets recorded too. For example, a therapist was listening to a child describe a recent ritual abuse incident. When the therapist tried to find out about what happened, the four-year-old child replied, "You already know. You were there!" In that case, the perpetrators knew what the therapist looked like. They dressed someone up like her to make it seem that the therapist was a member of the perpetrator group. The abuse was carried out with the look-alike sitting in a darkened part of the room.

The therapist encouraged the child to go ahead and tell her what she could remember. As the child described things, she came to realize that the therapist look-alike never came very close to the child during the abuse, and never said anything. Other perpetrators pointed to the look-alike, and told the child that the therapist was part of their group, but she did not come into a well-lighted area, where the child could see her very clearly. As the child reexamined what her mind was telling her, she figured out it had been a trick. Mind control tricks get recorded, very accurately, during the original event, and need to be looked at carefully enough to get to the truth. The child was abused by a group, and their attempt to sabotage therapy by staging a ritual with a therapist look-alike did not work. The precision of the memory provided enough details to expose the trick.

Other types of distortion which can accompany dissociated memories include time and place problems, fatigue-related clarity, and sequence-of-the-event difficulties. These are only peripheral, nonimportant parts of the memories. They in no way cast doubt on the validity of the memory. The essential elements get recorded, along with the peripheral distortions. Something bad happened, and we cannot honestly dismiss the memory just because some peripheral details may be doubtful.

When there is a car wreck, people debate the details endlessly. It may never be known exactly what happened, but no one says there was no wreck! That is the way memories work—even if we never get all the details right, we cannot ignore the basic truth. Something bad happened.

Please look at figure 1, which shows the different pathways taken by repressed and dissociated memories. Dissociation happens instantly, and repression takes place later, over a period of time. This figure illustrates how memories are recorded and helps explain how memories are recovered. They are recovered in the same way they were recorded. Dissoci-

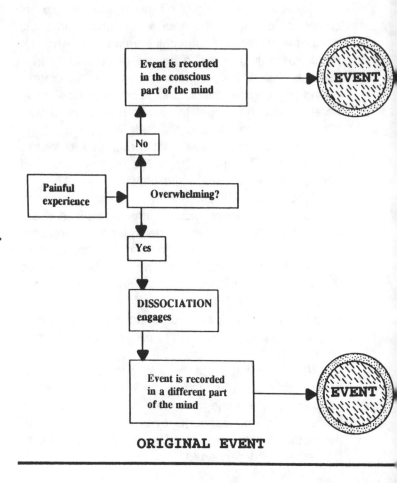

ORIGINAL EVENT

Figure 1: REPRESSION

Accurate Recording   Original Distor

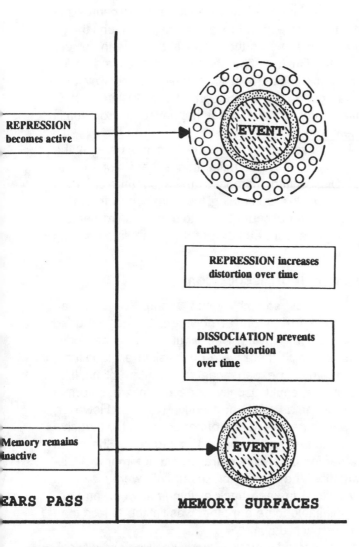

REPRESSION
becomes active

EVENT

REPRESSION increases
distortion over time

DISSOCIATION prevents
further distortion
over time

Memory remains
inactive

EVENT

EARS PASS

MEMORY SURFACES

AND DISSOCIATION

istortion from Repression

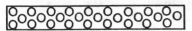

ated memories were lost instantly, and they came back instantly. They appear frozen in time, as though things are still the same as they were at the time they were recorded. On the other hand, repressed memories come back a little at a time, which is the way they were forgotten. As the person retraces his life history, earlier perceptions of what happened are gradually remembered.

Repressed memories usually come back in the first person—they seem like things that "happened to me." Dissociated memories are altogether different. They seem like something that "happened to some- one else"—an account being told in the third person. They have never been part of the person's conscious history.

An Example of Dissociation

Gina knew something was wrong. Powerful feel- ings came to her out of nowhere. Images intruded while she was driving. She would experience bodily pains for which there were no feasible explanations. These intrusive experiences would interrupt her life, though she could usually get back into her normal living routine as a wife and working mother. However, following a trauma to one of her children, the intrusive experiences became more of a problem. She could lose her job if her concentration did not improve. Dis- orientation and missing blocks of time were making it very difficult to keep track of things at work, and en- ergy available to be a mother was limited to less than an hour each day.

She entered therapy already knowing she dissoci- ated. Having read my first two books, she had talked with her husband and friends about how precisely her life is described by them. Blocks of her life history were missing, she often suffered from instant headaches and inappropriate bodily pains, and her mind was switching from one topic to another so often that she could lose track of what she was doing.

Despite these difficulties, she was able to remain focused at work most of the time by staying in a bright, engaging mood. She also was very active as a member of the worship team at her church, where she performed many Sundays, clearly enjoying the musical experience. But sometimes, the part of her which showed up at home just wanted to go to bed and stay there.

This illustrates what dissociative people go through. They struggle day after day, but appear mostly problem-free to the outside world. Entering therapy is a "good news—bad news" thing for them. The dissociative framework clears up many confusing points in their lives, which is good news. But, the truth about the abuse in their lives is bad news.

Even though I know the course of therapy will not be easy for people like Gina, I also know dissociation is a very effective coping mechanism. Early in therapy the decision needs to be made not to dismantle the dissociative mechanism. It can be used in a beneficial way. In Gina's case, it was important to keep her "career part," her "housewife part," and her "creative part" in their daily routine. We wanted Gina to let her strong parts stay in charge of her life, so wounded parts were not needed in the complicated matters of daily life. Wounded "child parts" learned to wait for safe times, and the "adult parts" kept life operating in a healthy fashion. That is using dissociation adaptively, so the patient can continue being successful in her daily life. Repression is not that adaptive.

Gina has trouble thinking clearly about her conscious memories of childhood abuse. Her parents were more than just dysfunctional. They were abusive in particular ways she has always remembered. At times, she would not be allowed to leave the house for weeks, maybe months, and those episodes are part of her life which she has always remembered. The mother was eventually convicted of child abuse, and was imprisoned. A parent like that could carry out acts of terror and violence. Gina's worst memories, which were dissociated, were very difficult for her to accept. Dissociated memories are practically always that way—not only do they seem to have happened to someone else, they are repulsive. One would hope they are not true.

Two things have helped her know that the dissociated memories have a basis in fact: She remembers enough about her parents to know they were abusive, and she sees behaviors in her life which are consistent with dissociation. She remembers some sections of an abusive childhood, and certain behaviors in her adult life suggest dissociation. This gives her confidence that the emerging memories are the sections in her childhood which have been missing.

As a therapist and a human being, I wish very much that the memories were not true. When she begins to open up in my office about flashbacks which keep intruding into her mind, I cannot block myself off from my own feelings. I would like to be able to tell her something like, "Well, maybe it didn't really happen that way." But, that would be dishonest. Her problems are consistent with those memories; the years of intrusive feelings, missing blocks of time, and flashbacks make it unmistakable that she has shown signs of dissociation during her whole adult life. Her husband has known her since she was a teenager and can attest that everything she says about her abuse-related behavior patterns, and about her parents, is true.

Nor can I dismiss the evidence in front of me during therapy sessions. There are switches in her posture and in her voice. Very strong feelings come over her instantly. She relives abusive events.

Yet, even in the most difficult part of her therapy, she continues to stay on task—she really wants to overcome the effects of childhood abuse. The drive to be healthy, which I have observed in dissociators many times, is "the clincher" in affirming her diagnosis. Her deep desire to get well cannot be overlooked by those who wonder if she is telling the truth.

I have spent many hours with her, and know she is a truthful person. She does not seek negative attention in any way I have seen. When she talks about her memories, she does not dwell on the details. Neither of us wants to spend more time than necessary on the repulsive aspects of the memories. Gina does not want to grovel; she wants to get better. Her husband, her friends, and I can see wonderful qualities in her—qualities that are inconsistent with "making up false memories."

Pseudomemories

When people describe to me what they mean when they use the term *false memory*, it turns out that they are describing something therapists often call a *pseudomemory*. When people are suggestible, they may believe that something about them is true simply because somebody told them so. Such a person could conceivably believe untrue things under the guidance of a therapist. I stress the word *conceivably* because I am not aware of any such person.

Therapists with standard training in multiple personality disorder/dissociative identity disorder (MPD/DID) assessment will not make the mistake of misdiagnosing a suggestible person as a dissociator. Assessment includes looking for dissociative symptoms which are present, and seeking evidence that those symptoms were noted earlier in the client's life.[5] If dissociative behavior patterns are present, and if those patterns have been evident in the past, it should be

understood that memories of childhood abuse are likely
to appear in adulthood. However, if a client describes
abuse memories without evidence of lifelong dissociative behavior patterns, a pseudomemory may be indicated.

Fantasy and Therapy

False memory-fighting groups have charged that
clients uncover abuse memories because the therapist uses fantasy material incorrectly. *Regression
therapy*, *trance states therapy*, and *hypnosis-induced
memories* are terms used to misinform the public about
what really goes on in therapy. I do not use regression, trances, or hypnosis.

It is possible to use fantasy material incorrectly in
therapy. I believe it is a mistake to lead a client in
"guided imagery" because it may suggest particular
things happened to them which did not. Therapists
are not supposed to tell clients what happened—the
client is supposed to do the telling. Therapists cannot
change what happened to a client by changing his
fantasy life. Mind manipulations do not aid people in
real life. My office is on the thirteenth floor, which is
the highest floor of the building. If I imagine the eleva-
tor will take me to floor fourteen, that is not going to
make it happen. That illustrates the difficulty with fantasy work. Therapy can only take a person to a place
consistent with reality. Anything which is only imagi-
nary will not become a stable part of the person's life.

Dissociated and repressed memories make their
way from the unconscious into conscious awareness
through predictable patterns, and the therapist does
not make it happen through mind control. The therapist does know what patterns of emerging memories
look like, and can create the proper conditions for
memories to surface safely.

Here is an example. Yesterday morning, a client

told me she has been feeling drugged part of the time at work during the last few days, and on the way to my office her body was feeling sharp pains in areas where abuse happens. A memory was making its way into her consciousness. Quietly in my office, with her eyes open part of the time, she told me what she was seeing and hearing. She saw hooded people through the eyes of a young girl, was told to drink something, soon became very sleepy, and was abused. The process was predictable: Painful memories emerged spontaneously when the conditions were safe. They longed to be healed. Therapists usually do not have to prod memories—they are near the surface and just need permission to emerge. That is not fantasy work. It is remembering.

Her body remembered being drugged, then her mind remembered the event. After that session she no longer felt drugged at work, and her body pains stopped. That is not suggestion. It is healing.

Charges and Countercharges

I used to work in a child guidance clinic, where the atmosphere was charged with fear about legal issues which surrounded our work with families. Divorced parents brought charges against each other. Children were caught in the middle, and so were therapists. We tried to protect the children while half-truths and outright lies were exchanged by the parents. I know what it is like to see people in custody disputes, where the truth is not nearly as important as winning. Often, the warring parties went public with their charges, which is a fierce battle tactic. Not only was it hard for children to figure out the truth, but the charges and countercharges, sharpened by coaching from lawyers, made everyone uncertain about the parents' honesty. There were many battles, but few winners. Everybody suffered.

How different it is for me today. None of my dissociative clients wants to bring charges, and none is going to court. The last thing they want is a public spectacle. They want no battle. They wish to keep away from the fighting if they can.

Maybe there are people somewhere who would like to get revenge by drumming up false accusations against their parents. Maybe certain people find the excitement of public accusation hard to resist. Maybe there are people who make up far-fetched stories to tell their therapists—perhaps there are even people willing to pay one hundred dollars an hour to entertain therapists with disgusting tales. But I have not met those people.

The people who come to me as clients are much different than that. They are people with integrity, who only want to recover. Not one of them uses therapy to get revenge. They are not manufacturing stories as they go along. They are just being honest with their families, friends, and therapists about what is going on inside of them.

They are not shaping their lives to fit something they heard on TV. Their lives have displayed dissociative symptoms for many years before they heard about multiple personality disorder and before they heard about terrorized children.

Their memories are upsetting and hard to believe. That does not make the memories false. History is full of accounts where people have done upsetting, hard-to-believe things to other people. It is surprising for me to watch people try to deny that horrible things happen. They must have flunked history, and they must not read newspapers. The memories brought into my office should not be dismissed simply because they are upsetting.

It is precisely because the memories are disturbing that these people sought help in the first place. That help is seriously threatened if their memories are dismissed or minimized by charges that they are making everything up.

A person I am working with received a you-must-be-having-false-memories letter from her sister, just last week. She told me, "I cannot explain in words how much that hurts." The progress she has made in therapy has been trashed in the letter, overruled by a person who knows practically nothing about therapy. The sister claims she has new information from an article she read about false memories. The letter even invites my client to get together sometime soon to straighten everything out. It is outrageous—this sister has not even talked with my client in about a year, and has no idea what is happening in her therapy or in her life! My client needs her support but is getting hurt instead. Progress in therapy almost always stalls until family and friends are supportive. The truth surfaces when conditions are safe.

We now turn to the process of getting to the truth.

CHAPTER 3:

"My Wife Has False Memories"

How Do People Discover What Is Accurate about Memories?

A man sent a message on my voice mail, and I got back to him the next day. He told me his wife had been in therapy for about two years, and the situation he described to me seemed familiar, one that often stumps therapists. His voice was strained and high-pitched. "Will you please evaluate my wife? She has false memories," he said.

He had encouraged her to drop out of therapy, since they both believed therapy was not solving her problems. The man was extremely upset, because he had been unable to find out what could possibly happen in therapy that would insert bad memories into her mind.

His questions came out one after the other, and I hardly had a chance to reply. When he finally paused I told him it would probably be a good idea for me to talk with them both in my office. They live about two hours away, but despite the distance, he set up an appointment.

She had initially sought therapy for anxiety and depression, which had recently become much worse.

When that therapy began, pictures started showing up in her mind and feelings came out, but the therapist did not know what to do. He stayed with the case and tried to learn about dissociated memory therapy by going to a seminar. That helped therapy become more effective for a while. The first memories were from her teen years, and those seemed to receive some healing.

Then, memories from a younger age came out, with much stronger feelings. They were more difficult to deal with, and the methods which had been successful with the teen memories did not bring the early childhood memories any peace. Voices and pictures from those early events made frequent intrusions into her mind. She worked very hard to manage her life more effectively. She kept her job and spent much of her extra time working on the memories. She wrote them down in a journal as they came to her, including some pictures of torture and horrific abuse. She was appalled and confused. Some of the pages she remembered writing, but she had no idea where other pages had come from, especially the ones with the drawings depicting abuse.

Her life became full of anxiety, and the therapist seemed to become more distant. He had gone from interested, to involved, to very involved, to giving up. It was all she could do to keep her job and stay calm after sensing his abrupt abandonment.

I scanned the chaotic pages of that journal. There were at least seven different handwriting styles, and sometimes the handwriting would change right in the middle of a sentence. As we looked at the pages together in my office, she pointed out the ones she did not remember writing.

It was apparent to me that parts of her wanted very much to get their issues dealt with. That is the reason the parts were all trying to write their stories in the journal—they each wanted to get some help.

She was a person whose memories of abuse and behavior patterns fit together consistently—the diagnosis was multiple personality. Sixteen of the eighteen items on the Dissociation Indicators Checklist came out positive. (See appendix B.) As I went over the questions on the list with them, I observed she was switching among quite a few personalities. That was what confirmed the diagnosis—she dissociated in front of me. I even met some of the personalities who had written in the journal, and they explained what they had written.

There was lots of switching, and statements were made that none of this had happened, followed by other child parts telling me about the abuse. Back and forth she went. Denial and affirmation. Things really happened just that way. No. They didn't happen at all. If maybe things did happen, she hoped it wasn't her parents, but it could have been her parents. Then there was a very strong affirmation of how loving and attentive the father had been to her. "It wasn't him! It wasn't the mother! I don't know who it was." The situation was confusing to the woman, and it was confusing to her former therapist. It certainly was confusing to the husband.

One of the benefits of asking her husband to join us was that he saw, for the first time, what a switch between her parts looked like. Unfortunately, the former therapist had not included him in therapy; he had not seen the journal; and he had no training in how to relate to her parts. His questions were finally getting some answers.

But, the thing this couple wanted to know was, how to deal with the "false memories." I could only tell them that I was observing dissociation, and that the journal entries are very much like other accounts given by people who dissociate. I said that so far, I had not seen anything I considered false.

The husband was surprised and said he had read this kind of memory is always false. He was baffled. The wife remained quiet, while the husband and I discussed things. He could accept what I was saying, but since she was alternately affirming and denying the memories, he could not believe they were true. She couldn't even believe that.

It was a relief for them to hear that her downhill slide could be stopped. I explained that therapists who are relatively inexperienced at treating dissociative disorders need input from other therapists at times, and the previous therapist should have found a colleague from whom to get additional input.

This woman's experience in therapy parallels many other dissociator's experiences, in that she tried to work on too many emotionally charged memories at once. They came into her awareness together, too forcefully. The result was a lot of rapid switching between the parts, with heightened anxiety and depression. The injured child parts were trying to tell their stories, but were being blocked by other parts who were loyal to the family. "Daddy was guilty, no he wasn't." With stress that high, there would be no resolution. Things needed to calm down first.

This couple had come in for an evaluation, and I was ready to give my opinion. I told them she had a dissociative disorder, and the stress of intensive therapy had led to depression. Her denial that the memories were true can be explained in this way: The rapid dissociative process we observed often occurs after long periods of high stress. The anxiety and depression, which arise from the switching, produce enough instability to produce internal disagreement over the memories.

This evaluation was the start of her return to therapy, with a much improved prognosis. Last I heard, she was taking anti-depressant medication, was still on the job, and had learned to slow down the memory work. Her life was still difficult, but no longer marked by internal bickering. The anti-depressant medication and the slower therapy pace led to less frequent switching and better healing for the memories, and there was less distortion while recovering the memories.

This woman got back on track in her therapy, but it could have turned out otherwise. If her husband had placed a phone call to one of her family members instead of to me, can you imagine what may have happened? The family could have blamed the therapist for implanting false memories. The woman's memories of abuse would have been pushed down again, at least temporarily. And, since suffering does not stay down for very long, her troubles would no doubt have resurfaced, and she would probably be worse off than ever.

The conclusion that the memories are false could have led to public allegations and the renunciation of her therapist in a headline-grabbing trial. Soon she would have found herself with the same problems, but therapists would no longer want to get involved for fear of getting sued! It appears that when clients decide their memories must be false, a return to the calm life they had hoped for simply does not happen.

It is better in the long run to help people discover what is accurate about their memories than it is to let others convince them the memories must be false. Confusion can be cleared up, to a great extent.

Problems with Memory Recall

Once in a while, helpful material comes to me unexpectedly, and I know it is more than a coincidence. A few months ago, I was quietly reviewing some notes while waiting in an airport. A therapist whom I had supervised when she was still an intern walked by. I called her name, "Jan!," and she jerked as though she had run into an electric fence.

We found we would be on the same flight and made arrangements to sit together. Jan's first disclosure to me was that she had been molested by a former therapist, and had placed a complaint against him. She explained that she had seen him at an airport the last time she flew and was just thinking about him when I called her name. She almost flashed back to memories about the other therapist.

But, running into me at this airport was a good thing. She said she really wanted to tell me about some things she had gone through in the last five years. The second disclosure was that she discovered she was a "multiple." I had met weekly with her as a supervisor, we co-led a group for a year, and it crossed my mind then that she might be a dissociator. But, I found it unnecessary to pursue that train of thought with her five years earlier because she was a very good intern. Nothing I saw then would confirm she was dissociating. Looking back, I believe she had been living in her healthy parts at our clinic.

Jan and I had a great time together during the flight. As she opened up to me about her history of family abuse which had come to light, and about the course of her therapy, I realized that her story illustrated the notes I had been going over in the airport. I was catching a flight to present a seminar concerning uncovering memories, and was looking for examples of two common problems. The chance meeting with Jan was very helpful: Her account was exactly what I was looking for. Here is how Jan's experiences fit into what I was preparing to explain at the seminar.

Problem #1: Dissociators Are Suggestible

Knowing that dissociation starts because of abuse, helps us understand the problem I was trying to explain. Many of these people automatically have a high need to please others, in order to avoid any possibility of offending the people they love. Staying "nice" has kept them safe at times. Keeping this in mind, therapists need to be careful not to suggest to the client what might have happened. The client may try to please the therapist by choosing to believe that whatever the therapist suggested must be true. A vulnerable person does not want to displease the therapist!

Jan told me that while a difficult memory was opening up in her therapy, one friend kept on asking if the abuser was her father. She already knew her grandfather had abused her at other times, and was pretty sure he was the perpetrator in the emerging memory, but her friend's question about her father stopped that memory from being clarified any further. She was hesitant to contradict her friend or even to ask the friend to stop pressing the issue about her father, so she consciously blocked working on that memory and had no clear evidence as to whether the perpetrator was her father or her grandfather. A few months later she went back to work on that memory and became aware of the specifics which told her the perpetrator was the grandfather. Her therapy got back on track.

During the months between the friend's persistent questions and the resolution of the memory, Jan told me she had some difficulty whenever she was with her father. She could not look into his eyes. There was no reason to accuse him, but I wonder if similar cases sometimes result in accusation. Such an accusation would be damaging and false.

In Jan's case, the pain caused by the friend's persistence was minimal, but friends of dissociators, and especially their therapists, need to be very careful not to ask leading questions. It is enough to listen and to have the dissociator be the one to say what is going on inside. They are suggestible, so do not suggest to them what happened.

As Jan and I talked, she was happy to add that she never really thought her father was a perpetrator, and following the proper resolution of that memory, she has enjoyed her relationship with her father again. It is reassuring for me to know that the course of therapy can be corrected after a mistake.

Problem #2:
Memories Should Not Be Challenged

Another setback in Jan's therapy occurred when a different friend started to doubt her own memories. The friend concluded that memories of ritual abuse could not be true, and became insistent that all bad memories must be false. Even though Jan's memories involved no ritual abuse, the friend challenged their accuracy. Evidently, she was hoping that Jan would renounce her memories too.

Some news reports about false memories were receiving attention at that time, and Jan seriously reconsidered whether she wanted to stay in therapy. Lots of clients have similar reactions to false memory "news." One person put it this way: "I am forced to be counterfeit. I cannot share what happened with my friends [because they believe the reports about false memories]. It is unfair that I am shamed into silence." What a loathsome development—she was shamed into silence about her abuse as a child and now the same thing is happening as an adult, thanks to the false memory reports.

Jan was effectively silenced about her memories. Life would be much easier without the extra shame, so I can understand her desire to drop the memory work. But, Jan wanted to overcome the problems in her life. When she avoided the memories, she found her problems became worse. She decided to stick with the work she was doing in therapy.

On the plane, Jan's face was aglow as she shared that her life is better than ever. Now she remembers what happened, and would no longer have any difficulty with suggestibility or with being challenged. Things happened, and they are in the past. She has gone beyond the pain and uncertainty, which would not be the case if she had believed the false memories articles.

Of particular concern to me is the position taken by a false memory-fighting group. They state they know—without asking the client or the therapist—that a memory of a traumatic experience is "objectively false" if recovery of the memory results in personality and lifestyle changes. Do they think people are supposed to stay the same? If a traumatic experience is handled properly in therapy, changes in personality and lifestyle are precisely the outcome hoped for! Recovery from traumatic memories should produce changes. Adults are expected to create new directions in their lives when they overcome their problems, even if their families do not approve.

It makes more sense to carefully examine each client's perspective when considering the objectivity of a memory, than to simply invoke this group's categorical, groundless denial. An abused person has trouble when confronted with that kind of a challenge.

Here is an example of how a client's progress has made it possible to withstand such groundless denial.

The mother phones: "Where's my cute little Penny? [Penny is 40!] Why don't you come celebrate Christ-

mas with the family anymore?" Then the mother becomes very emotional and says Penny's changes
began when she started seeing "that therapist." She
backs up her charge by citing a false memory syndrome article: "You have 'child alienation syndrome'
[a term which has been manufactured by this particular group] since you have been in therapy. I am sending you some articles so you can see what the therapist is doing to you, and we can put all this behind us."

Therapists call that kind of message a "double-
bind." There is no right answer. It is also called "crazy-
making," and can be very damaging. Children who
grow up in double-binding homes develop unhealthy
symptoms. A double-binding challenge to memories
which are already difficult, may throw the person back
into a double-bound child position, and cause the
unhealthy symptoms to appear once again. It is hard
for a client to maintain a new direction in life, when
faced with such a challenge.

But Penny sizes up the mother's ploy, and re-
sponds appropriately: "That is what my life has always
been like. I can't talk to you! I can't please you! Our
family has always had to stay quiet about difficult issues, but I'm never going back to the 'rule of silence.'
I need support, not opposition."

The rift between accusing parents and an adult
child who is building a healthy life becomes wider in
response to double-binding challenges. The pathway
to reconciliation is not through challenge. It is through
support. I would like to hear parents say they are
going to be supportive through the recovery process,
and offer unconditional acceptance.

Consistency between People

Most of the time when memories of extreme abuse
come up, the client has great difficulty trusting the
memory. It does not seem true, and the hope endures

for a long time that there may be another way to explain things. Hearing the therapist say that others have seen the same things is somewhat helpful. It is also sometimes helpful to read other survivors' accounts.[1]

I often mention to survivors that we would expect many variations and different kinds of abuse situations in peoples' stories, if memories were just being produced randomly. But, what I hear are accounts that are pretty much the same. I hear nothing about extraterrestrial abductions, or other more interesting scenes that could pass through a mind with rich fantasies. People describe the same scenes, with the same kind of suffering, and the same kinds of mind control tricks.

For example, when a child personality's memory includes people speaking in unison, saying words not understandable, standing around a fire in black robes, it helps the child to know that a lot of other children have told me they heard chanting too. Kids tell me about fires and black robes all the time, and I can believe them. It is vital for them to be believed since they were specifically told by the perpetrators that their experiences would not be believed.

Internal Consistency

Confidence in the recovery process is strengthened when there is consistency among the memories. When the person's memories of abuse happen in the same circumstances, the memories appear to fit together. Finding such a pattern helped Joan see that her emerging memories could be accurate.

After uncovering three memories of extreme abuse, Joan noticed that all took place indoors, at about age four. Two were in rooms without windows, and one included being taken down some stairs. All seemed to have taken place in a basement, and, although she could not be certain, Joan sensed they took place in a church. That led to some fruitful detective work.

External Evidence

Getting on the phone with her family members, Joan was told that she had spent a few weeks of summer vacation with friends when she was three and four years old. It was in a different state, and Joan had no conscious recall of the visits. One of her aunts told Joan she remembered some people down the street who would pick the young Joan up and take her to a local church for vacation Bible school. None of the relatives knew anything about the church, except its name and location. Something inside of Joan seemed to know that this was the arena of her abuse.

Later that year, Joan went on a family vacation which included a few days in that town. The library revealed some things about the history of that church including names and dates, which supported her suspicions. She found the location of the church, which had been remodeled into a large house. The family who lived there let her go down into the basement, and Joan found it was laid out just the way her memories had told her. She recognized that the top of the stairway to this basement is where one memory began. She had made a floor plan of the basement ahead of time, and that basement fit the floor plan. Her memories were given support—she found the place where they happened.

Does that prove anything? Yes—that her memories came from somewhere. Would that stand up in court? No. Did the trip provide support for the difficult work she was doing in my office? Yes. Supportive external evidence is helpful. Three pieces of evidence add up to make a very powerful case for Joan: Her behaviors show a lifetime of dissociation, her memories are internally consistent, and they describe the location of the abuse. For Joan, it was important to have as much evidence as possible. External evidence meant she could have more confidence to seek the support she needed from her friends. Without that support, it would have been very difficult for her to deal with the abuse she was discovering in her childhood.

I wish all my clients had that many sources of evidence for their memories. Many times there is not nearly as much external evidence as there was in the case for Joan. Those people need to develop confidence in other sources of evidence—the knowledge that there is consistency among peoples' memories and a growing awareness that there is internal consistency. But, even when external evidence is found, the process of uncovering the memory is painful, and it is always very difficult to get close to the feelings being uncovered.

Uncovering Dissociation

Dora is a middle-aged woman who began to get in touch with disturbing feelings for the first time while she was talking to a woman she knew from her church. Initially, she discovered only anxiety, with no known cause. As Dora let herself get closer to the anxiety, she unexpectedly got three internal clues about the event that was producing the anxiety. She saw a big yellow advertising chicken on top of a building; she sensed it was near the place where her family had vacationed every summer during her childhood; and she heard a person's nickname, Slim.

Dora had never uncovered a memory before, knew nothing about memory recall, and had never known anyone named Slim! Things were getting very confusing to her, and the anxiety was getting worse. Martha was the therapy partner of a different dissociative client of mine, and told Dora it would be a good idea to talk about these three clues "in Dr. Friesen's office." Martha sensed a dissociative episode was about to be uncovered.

So, Martha introduced me to Dora, and stayed to be her therapy partner. A few sessions were spent getting to understand Dora's life history, and then we took a look at the three clues. As she let the pictures come to her, Dora's mind got in touch with the disso-ciated event. She was age twelve again, and her bare feet could feel the coarse gravel alongside the build-ing which had the yellow chicken on top. Slim was there, urging her to comply with his wishes. That was where the anxiety hit, warning her not to let the rest of the memory come forth. He molested her, and after-wards, she remembered feeling hot and dirty. She also remembered telling her brother what happened, and he told her not to tell anyone else.

Martha was the right person to include as her partner. The memory at age twelve was more than a memory—it was another part of her, and that person-ality got to know Martha in my office. The young Dora received from Martha what she had been seeking from her brother—comfort, protection, and someone to share her shame and outrage. That is why memories emerge—to resolve conflicts and feelings. It was good for Dora to receive support from Martha and from me in order to resolve her feelings.

When her brother told Dora to stay quiet, she dis-sociated and split off from this event. No wonder things were so precise in Dora's memory. It was as though the event, which had taken place twenty-five years earlier, had just happened in my office. All the sounds, bodily experiences, and feelings—everything was so clear. There was no mistaking that this was what some people call a flashback. Martha had seen flashbacks before. Together, we oriented the twelve-year-old part to changes in her present life, and helped the adult part of Dora understand what she needed to know about memory recall. We told her we believed the memory may have been accurate, and supported her when she said she wanted to look for external evidence.

Before the next session, she had a meeting with her brother, and he said he remembered the episode. He remembered Slim and the building with the yellow chicken. He even apologized for coaching her to keep quiet. It was a family rule not to talk about negative things, so Dora and the brother were dutifully following that rule, as would be expected. The family was supposed to talk only about things that were "nice," and everything was supposed to look "normal." Nonetheless, in 1993, the time had come to start breaking the rules. The brother and another sister joined Dora in talking about the negative things that had happened in their childhoods. The "yellow chicken" event was only the tip of the iceberg.

The shame and outrage were properly resolved for the younger part of Dora, and the anxiety which had previously protected her from those two unwanted feelings was no longer necessary. We hope that will happen when traumatic memories emerge.

Sometimes, though, mistakes can be made which hinder the resolution of feelings. The whole truth about memory recall must include the fact that well-meaning therapists can be misleading at times. We cannot look at memories as all true or all false. Nor should we try to see therapists as correct or incorrect in all they do. Therapists certainly can make errors. Here is how Martha and I helped her other therapy partner deal with a mistake made by a former therapist.

When a Therapist Makes a Mistake

Martha has devoted herself to the growth of her church friends. For about five years, she has been working with me and with other therapists, to help the friends find resolution for their feelings. A recognized counselor at her church, Martha has led programs and has developed different problem-solving groups in addition to being a therapy partner for a number of people.

She was a partner for Carolyn, who was having a great deal of trouble with an emerging memory. It was satanic ritual abuse of the worst kind. Carolyn was telling Martha and me what she was seeing.

I knew that Carolyn had been in treatment with another therapist and that Martha had been her therapy partner there too. But I did not know that this was a memory which had already been dealt with by the other therapist, and I did not know that Martha had been present to witness how the other therapist had handled the memory of Satanic ritual abuse.

Here is what happened in my office. Carolyn detailed the sequence of events, to the point where she was placed on a table. The adult Carolyn was telling me about the memory through the eyes of a younger part. So far, the things I was hearing were not different from accounts of abuse I had heard from other clients. But, all at once, she started describing things which did not add up for me. Carolyn said she was seeing Jesus coming into the middle of the ritual, picking her up off the table, taking her outside, and putting her up in a tree. I asked her to explain.

The adult Carolyn stopped the memory work momentarily and told me the former therapist had created the "Jesus rescue" right in the middle of the memory work. That therapist was mixing fantasy and reality, and Carolyn tried to believe the fantasy account with all her heart, including the ending which had the younger Carolyn up in a tree.

Martha confirmed that this was exactly what happened. She remembered what the other therapist said and did. The other therapist would often take an emerging memory and make it "turn out better" by suggesting other endings. She had created the Jesus rescue. She told the younger part of Carolyn to stay up in the tree, where she would be safe. But, Carolyn told me the younger part was actually afraid of heights, and would love to come down out of the tree!

After explaining to Carolyn that memories are not to be interrupted if they are going to be resolved, I encouraged her to go back to the place where the other therapist superimposed the fantasy rescue on top of the dissociated memory. I encouraged her to let the rest of the memory come forward. We found that the part of the memory the other therapist had cut off contained a conflict which needed resolution. The perpetrators made her do some things which they claimed made her "bad." God would never love her, and she would always be bad, at least that is what she was told at the end of the memory.

But now we had the whole memory, and we could address the conflict that needed resolution. We knew what the most troublesome thing was in this memory—the belief that she was a bad person whom God could never love. The nagging sense that God could not love her had seriously impaired her self-image for years, but was about to be reversed.

Martha and I helped the younger part understand the truth about God's love. As the Bible says, "Nothing in all creation will ever be able to separate us from the love of God" (Rom. 8:38-39). Peace came to the adult Carolyn and to her younger part as the truth set in. The curse in the memory was banished. Her conflict disappeared right in front of us. She began to accept love from God and from Martha. Now she knows that she is not bad. She is loved by God. She will always be loved by God.

Looking back at that session, I believe some important lessons can be learned. (1) Memories can be altered by well-meaning therapists. (2) If a memory has been altered, that does not mean the whole memory should be called false. (3) It is possible to go back, take another look, and discover how the mistake took place. These are three important lessons for therapists, and for those who want to understand memory recall better. The lesson that is most important to the client is this: (4) Resolution can be attained, even if mistakes were made.

The mind is magnificent. You can take it off track, but it can find the mistake and make its way back. Dissociation preserves events well enough to provide the details necessary to find the truth.

An Example: Evaluating Chloe's Memory

Whenever a memory surfaces, it needs to be evaluated in its context. This process can be complicated and may take some time because a client's description of a surfacing memory may be confusing to the listener, and the behavior may seem unnatural. A casual observer could easily conclude it is nothing more than terrific acting. Nonetheless, by carefully considering the circumstances, the memory's accuracy can be established.

Here is an illustration of how memories are brought up by outside events. It shows that when a memory emerges, painful material from the past is working its way into consciousness in order to find relief. During the evaluation process, the personality with the emerging memory needs to be handled gently. The therapist's goal is to promote understanding of the incoming material and to relieve some of the tension contained in it.

A Week Ago

Chloe has been working with me for over a year. We have found she has a fairly large number of personalities, and last week one of them challenged me in a way which suggested she had rehearsed what to say. This misled personality (M) had memorized sentences right out of a false memory pamphlet, which I had also read. She said she has no repressed memories and has made everything up.

I pointed out I had never told her any memories—she had told them to me. I continued to explain memory work to M by recounting to her the things that led her to begin therapy with me. Chloe's former therapist had met a new personality (N), who startled both Chloe and the therapist with some highly uncharacteristic behavior. N started buying and consuming cigarettes and beer, which appalled Chloe—she found cigarette smell on her breath, and was inexplicably under the influence of alcohol! N identified herself to the therapist with a different name, and would not answer to "Chloe." This had taken place after more than two years of therapy for depression, without any indication there were other personalities. N spoke to the former therapist as though he should know about the other personalities, but since nothing like this had ever happened in his office, he did not know what to do. Multiple personality would seem the obvious diagnosis, even though he had no appropriate training in the matter. He asked if I would become her therapist, since he knew I had some experience treating multiple personality.

As we spoke, it seemed M knew about the former

therapist, but could not remember just how she had begun therapy with me. The details were not available to her, so she lost her self-assurance about having no repressed memories. It appeared she was willing to learn from me, but was also trying to rely on what she had read about false memory syndrome. I wanted to help M understand from her own experience, what memory work is like and how dissociation can be identified. She deserved a thorough explanation. She had been misled.

We agreed to pray about discovering the truth. After a brief prayer, dissociation took her into a younger personality (Y). I invited her husband into the room to meet Y. A few minutes later we got back to M, who was surprised to find him sitting across the room. When I asked if she remembered him coming in she said nothing. I reminded her we had prayed for truth, and she dissociated right after that. M tried to find some other way to account for her behavior, but the husband's appearance in the middle of the session could only be explained as a dissociative experience. Becoming more and more uncomfortable, M could not stay. The ideas she had gleaned from the false memory pamphlet did not match her experience, so her tension rose and dissociation began to take place. The main personality, Chloe, replaced her, and I concluded the session by telling her about M and Y.

What Happened between Sessions

As we began this week's session, Chloe told me about a conversation she had, just after our last meeting, with her sister who has been influenced by false memory syndrome articles. The sister was hoping to find some traumas in Chloe's life which could explain her dissociative condition, so they talked of events which took place during Chloe's high school years. The family of origin had already decided Chloe's early memories must be false—they remember no childhood traumas. Despite Chloe's insistence she had not been given any clues to build a false memory around, the sister maintained they must be false even though family members had never asked about the memories. They had no idea what they were arguing about with her. Chloe told me that while her sister was arguing, a voice in her head was agreeing—M was joining the debate from inside!

The sister invited her to the next family gathering, even though the family now contradicts her. They are supposed to "agree to disagree" about her memories of being abused, and about whether serious problems in her life are based on nothing more than suggestibility. The sister's proposal is to act as though nothing has changed.

Those conditions would blame Chloe for making up every problem in her life, and for upsetting the family of origin. The family is supposed to get together and act as though everything is okay, which puts Chloe in the "crazy person" category. She would get zero respect under the "agree to disagree" conditions, and they are saying that things can go back to the way they were. That is precisely what she is afraid of—getting her feelings minimized again and continuing to be the object of blame for whatever is wrong.

This Week's Dreams

Right after telling me about the sister's phone call, Chloe told me about some dreams. The therapy process went right from the phone call to the dreams, so I suspected the dreams may have resulted from emotions stirred up by the phone call.

Chloe usually remembers no dreams at all, but following the talk with her sister, she started having dreams about a secret club in high school. In the dreams, she was baffled because she knew nothing about any club, but those around her treated her as though she knew she was one of the club leaders. After she finished telling me about the dreams, I mentioned that her sister had inquired about her high school years on the phone, which could explain where the dreams were coming from—conflicts from those years had been touched off. We decided to open up some therapy time to work on the dream material.

The Memory

I asked Chloe to talk to me from the personality who had the dreams. Her posture changed, and with eyes closed, she began asking me questions about a problem she was having. This personality (S) was in a group which required that dead bodies be kept a secret, but S was seeing somebody in an open casket with about four hundred people present. This was not a dream—S was telling me what she was seeing and hearing. It was a memory of trying to understand why it was allowed to have a dead body on public display, even though the group said that shouldn't happen. S was confused and upset as she asked why sometimes bodies were supposed to be a secret, but this time it is okay for so many people to look at the body.

I found out later in the session that an auto wreck had killed a high school friend. The public funeral was contrary to the group's requirement to be secretive. S did not talk to me about the group, only about how confusing it was to see a body openly displayed. S listened as I explained about the voices in her head, and about how she could feel less upset by working together with them. When I asked her to open her eyes to see how her body had grown up, she became confused because in her reality S was still a teenager. She dissociated because getting to know how things are today, twenty years later, was shocking. Chloe came back to the session once again.

Evaluating with Chloe

The tension from the dreams was becoming more understandable. Talking to the sister had brought up high school memories, and led her to a conflicted teen-age moment—when S ran out of the church in the middle of the funeral. The most recent event in S's short life had been the collision between her secret group's rules about corpses, and the reality of how other people treat the bodies of those who have died. This is a classic example of how seeking reality (the sister's phone call) results in finding a personality who is trying to understand reality. S had been struggling to figure out reality during the funeral. Chloe's sister and S were both trying to make sense out of confusing events.

Chloe told me all about the unexpected death of a young friend, and about how confusing it had been for her to find herself running away from the funeral. S's moments of confusion had ended as she left the church, and Chloe was unexpectedly brought into conscious control of the body. Chloe told me the friend's untimely death was something she remembered well, but she could not remember being inside the church at the funeral. We now know that S was the personality who attended the funeral.

I can imagine Chloe's sister observing that therapy session. When I asked to speak to the personality who had the dreams, she may have objected. When Chloe's eyes closed, her posture changed, and she began talking in a slightly different voice, the sister may have said she was making everything up. However, the evaluation was conclusive. The pieces fit together: We identified the outside event which prompted the memory (the phone call); we observed a dissociated personality trying to get relief from conflicted feelings (S); we found precisely when the dissociated event took place (as S was exiting the funeral, which is an unforgettable part of Chloe's life); and there was outside verification from the former therapist that Chloe has a history of dissociating. Her sister would be able to understand if she had been with us for the evaluation.

Discovering what is accurate about memories comes from listening. It comes from inviting the person to open up about conflicts, because relief is needed. It comes from letting things happen at their own pace, and not arguing about details which may at first make no sense. The evaluation often takes more time. Discovering the truth about memories helps— the client's life history has fewer unanswered questions, and tension is relieved. The resulting peace indicates the process has remained truthful. If it were based on falsehood, the memory work would be harmful instead of helpful.

People have a natural drive to understand their past, to resolve internal conflicts, and to seek a better life. If given a chance, the truth comes out and the resolution of conflicts can be enjoyed. The next chapter explains how dissociation can be a wonderful tool to serve the natural desire to live a healthier life.

CHAPTER 4:

The Public's Mistaken Beliefs

Is Multiple Personality Destructive or Adaptive?

Publishers like to schedule live radio interviews to promote their books. My publishers have arranged for me to discuss my books on quite a few shows. Practically all of the programs discuss different topics each day, and appeal to a large target group of listeners. Getting on lots of shows may be good for a book's publicity, but it is hard for me because I rarely know ahead of time how informed the host is, or what bias there may be in the way each show is packaged.

The publishers tell my answering machine when I will be getting a live phone interview, and that is about all I know. I usually receive a phone call from the radio station at the expected time, just before the program is to begin, and am put on hold. Then I quietly listen to their live local traffic news or to commercials being broadcast. Once the interview starts I try to figure out as soon as possible what direction the host wants to go.

Some hosts are quite knowledgeable about dissociative disorders, and are very articulate, while others know practically nothing. They are supposed to be helping the public take a close look at my material, but most of them have not even read my books. Some are stuck in stereotypical thinking from yesteryear.

On one occasion, a host started off the show with this question: "Dr. Friesen, can you tell us about the most unbelievable case you've had?" That opening question told me a lot about him. He was really asking, "Will you please reinforce my stereotype about how peculiar these people really are?" His mind had a pigeonhole for people who dissociate, right next to one labeled "people who give fantastic tales to tabloids." Perhaps he thought I would paint him verbal pictures of pathetic people who were hopelessly confused, and maybe even destructive.

I knew right away the program needed to stop feeding peoples' mistaken beliefs. I answered, "These are people who suffer silently, and I spend a lot of time with them while they go through their pain. Most of their daily lives are spent in healthy personalities. Many are high functioning people—M.D.s, therapists, teachers, musicians, nurses, county supervisors, and church leaders. Most acquaintances consider them to be very bright, creative, highly productive people. Many of their close friends have no idea they are multiples. They are loyal, compassionate people—the kind of people you would be glad to have as your friends."

Multiple personality disorder, or, using the newer term, dissociative identity disorder, is not an illness. MPD/DID is an effective defense mechanism; it protects in many ways, and has often been necessary for the person's survival. I want to help correct the widely accepted but incorrect perception that it is nothing more than a problem; it is actually a solution to problems. It is not an illness; it is a cure. It is not a curse; it is a gift to deal with difficult life circumstances. It is not crazy; it is a proper reaction to crazy life-events. It is adaptive, not destructive.

Dissociators develop a system of personality parts

to fend off danger and to keep life steady. The system regulates which parts are best suited to rotate out at any time, so the system can deal with practically anything.

Those of us who have a lot of contact with dissociators find the adaptivity hard to miss. For example, Betty's father molested her repeatedly in the middle of the night while she was a preschooler. The next morning, she would arise and face the day with no memory whatsoever of the incest. What a powerful tool dissociation was, to keep her life on track. Her life would have, no doubt, taken an unhealthy direction if she had needed to face each day carrying the feelings that result from remembering incest. Her self-image would have been seriously damaged, confidence destroyed, and she may have ended up lonely and unsuccessful. But, because dissociation protected her from having to deal with the incest as a child, we find her today as a woman who has a life. She has maintained a healthy self-image in many of her parts, even though some parts were damaged by the childhood events. Therapy is helping her deal with the early traumas, and she still has a life, preserved by the gift of dissociation.

Readers who would like to see how some personality systems look, are encouraged to rent or purchase this video: "Significant Others."[1] It is documentation of real people—there are no actors. As personality parts are interviewed on the tape, the viewer experiences the compelling evidence that these are wonderful people who are doing well, despite a difficult childhood. Their therapy is not easy and their lives are often a struggle, but they are endearing, thoughtful people.

Another resource which reveals the positive characteristics of dissociators is my second book, *More than Survivors: Conversations with Multiple Personal-*

ity Clients.[2] Nine dissociators are interviewed, two from my caseload, and the rest from different parts of the country. In the research that went into that book, and wherever I go, I keep finding the same thing. People who never thought of themselves as dissociators discovered they were, but that has not prevented them from living meaningful lives. Many are devoted to worthy causes. That is remarkable: They have endured major childhood traumas, and, not only are they overcoming the negative effects of the abuse, they are contributing to the well-being of others. They have a lot to give.

Understanding Multiple Personality Better

The father of modern psychology, Dr. Freud, gave us a good start in understanding peoples' minds. As a pioneer, he covered much new ground about a hundred years ago. But, even a good pioneer sometimes loses his way. As I understand it, Dr. Freud seemed to believe his clients were telling him the truth at about the turn of the century. A few years later, however, after his clients told him about their memories of incest, he came up with a new diagnosis: hysterical neurosis.

It appears Dr. Freud's powerful influence has had far-reaching effects on the way people have looked at recovered memories. The memories which he found hard to reconcile with the way he viewed things, were put into the "hysterical" category, which is what therapists who have been trained in his tradition have been doing ever since. He honestly concluded that memories of incest were the product of a hysterical mind.

That sounds all too familiar today. If a memory is disturbing to the listener, it goes into the "hysterical imagination"/ "false memory" category. Unfortunately, for the one with the memory, the listener stops listening too soon and does not hear the things which would lead to the conclusion that the memory may be true.

Freud's term, *hysterical neurosis*, has not held up to scrutiny, and has been dropped as a valid diagnosis. The *DSM-IV* has no mention of *hysteria* nor of *neurosis*. I believe that psychologists in this decade are sticking closer to the facts, and are better listeners than their predecessors. Having rejected the idea that minds are hysterical, today's therapists are in a better position to assess the accuracy of what clients tell them.

In the late 1970s, well-respected therapists started discovering that memories are more trustworthy than they were taught. These therapists began to observe a number of symptoms which helped them describe a syndrome: multiple personality disorder. Although there had been articles about that diagnosis for more than one hundred years, it was generally considered rare. In the 1940s, some researchers had even reached the conclusion that it was extinct. But, since the seventies, the way therapists think about dissociation has been evolving. We have learned a lot, and we are still learning.

Considering that the first book about treatment for multiple personality, *Minds in Many Pieces,* is so recent, I believe we have come a long way. By the early 1980s, therapists got together and began to share what they were learning about the dissociative condition and about treatment. They formed what is now the International Society for the Study of Dissociation (ISSD), and their membership includes hundreds of therapists who specialize in this area from all over the world.[4] These professionals have each invested thousands of hours and, together, have carried out hundreds of studies about MPD/DID. Another organization which is contributing to the understanding and treatment of MPD/DID is the Christian Society for the Healing of Dissociative Disorders.[5] There is a sizable increase in the number of recently released books about dissociative disorders, which reflects that much is being learned. During the last year alone about twenty good books were published.[6]

There is no excuse for people to maintain that MPD/DID is extinct, rare, or poorly understood. We need to invite those who are new to these ideas to call the ISSD, the CSHDD, and the Sidran Foundation for resources. People need to get up-to-date materials and do their homework.

Personality Systems Are Constantly Changing

One factor which reinforces stereotypical thinking is the belief that a system of personalities is bound to remain unchanged. I am not going to remain unchanged, you are not going to remain unchanged, and neither are they. We all take in new information, and grow as a result. Everybody is always changing, growing, and maturing.

Because I am a therapist, I probably am more attuned than most people to internal changes, but everybody knows that people are always in the process of change. Whoever comes into therapy is clearly seeking change, and that includes dissociators. Changes sought by dissociators usually require work in three areas: (1) managing the living environment, (2) improving cooperation within the system, and (3) seeking healing for wounded parts. The living environment must foster growth, so this area needs to receive attention first. Family and friends may need to be educated about the benefits of dissociation so they will more effectively foster the changes sought by the client. After support from the environment is in place, internal cooperation and healing can begin. Without understanding and encouragement from family and friends, cooperation and healing are unlikely to get very far. The outside world must be safe and supportive in order for the client to do the very difficult work inside.

Two types of changes can be expected during therapy for dissociators. (1) Personality parts work through problems and gain some maturity. Changes within the parts are almost always easy to detect. (2) Changes also occur in the system, as parts learn more about each other and establish better cooperation. System change affects each part, but is not as easy to observe.

Figure 2 illustrates some adaptive changes which develop during the initial stages of therapy. People in the living environments of the two clients portrayed there were very supportive, so therapy could stay focused on cooperation and healing. The changes shown on figure 2 indicate how therapy promoted healthy living in two ways—the parts made progress, and so did the system.

Ramona had been in therapy elsewhere for many years. Therapists and medical doctors had given her quite a few incorrect diagnoses. Whatever positive changes occurred for her during that time did not last. That is the way therapy is for dissociators—unless therapy is directed to the whole system, none of the parts improves very much.

Ramona's life was chaotic and disconnected. The chaos would not subside while her parts remained separated. After the correct diagnosis was finally reached, therapy got her "front line parts" acquainted and cooperating. That prepared her for changes that should last a lifetime. Her therapy is still underway, but the cooperation already achieved has made her life more effective than ever.

Dan's reason for seeking therapy was entirely dif-

STARTING PROBLEM   AFTER STABILIZATION

CHAOTIC, DISCONNECTED   COOPERATION IS ESTABLISHE

Case 1:   RAMONA

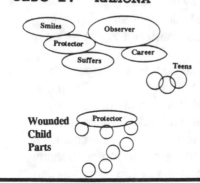
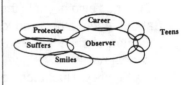

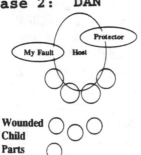
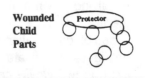

Wounded
Child
Parts

FEELINGS INTRUDE FROM   PARTS ARE IDENTIFIED AND
UNIDENTIFIED CHILD PARTS   INCLUDED IN DAILY LIFE

Case 2:   DAN

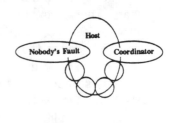

Wounded   Wounded
Child   Child
Parts   Parts

Figure 2:   CHANGES IN PERSONALITY SYSTEMS

ferent. He experienced very strong, unwanted sexual feelings and desires. It was almost as though he had no control over the way his sexuality was being lived out. He was desperate to see improvement in this area of his life. He was a married man and a father, but his desires were being pulled in a different direction. He came to me after another therapist recognized his dissociative symptoms, but did not know how to work with them.

Dan's therapy began by helping the front line parts identify each other, and to open up about each one's issues. Protector had been stopping everyone from getting near the wounded child parts who had been sexualized. They were the ones with sexual problems. When Protector learned that the wounded ones needed me to help them, he let me begin to work with them. Protector took the new name Coordinator, indicating his job is now to let the injured ones "out" to meet with helpful people. The part known as My Fault needed to let go of false guilt, for the sake of some child parts—guilt makes them very reactive. Host was the part in charge most of the time. The Host's anxiety subsided when he began to understand where the strong sexual feelings were coming from. His renewed confidence calmed the whole system. Dan's progress was off to a good start with the three front line parts working together and allowing wounded parts to seek help in my office.

Stereotypic Thinking Is Hard to Break

The prevailing beliefs about MPD are a major problem. Many people have already made up their minds about how weird and peculiar MPD is, and until they meet such a person, they tend to hold onto their stereotype very tightly. Talk shows may appear to portray multiple personality clients in a favorable light, but

usually end up fortifying peoples' mistaken perceptions. They miss a basic point: These are sensible
people. They would prefer to get their lives together
out of the public spotlight. It runs counter to their basic
fabric to go public about their very personal struggles.

Recently, I saw part of a major TV network program broadcasting a fictional tale about a multiple
who was a serial killer. I came away with my usual
observation about TV productions—they keep people
entertained at somebody's expense. Somebody has
to look bad. Sometimes it is airhead dads and sometimes it is dysfunctional families. This time it was
dissociators. The program got some of the facts right,
like the fact that MPD is usually the result of childhood
abuse, but the essential feature of multiplicity was
missed: It is adaptive, not destructive. Like other TV
accounts, this one reinforced mistaken beliefs.

One thing that particularly offended me about this
show was the "illness" stereotype. The lawyer who
represented the multiple proclaimed to a TV station
covering the serial killer story that we know beyond
the shadow of a doubt this is an illness. That is not the
case. Please take a look at the *DSM-IV*. MPD/DID is
a disorder. It is a style of coping which brings order to
a chaotic life. It is not an illness. The TV viewers who
believe that the lawyer-character was speaking correctly will consider MPD to be more like the plague
than a style of coping. Viewers were not told that
dissociation helps straighten out a difficult life.

I really cannot imagine any "personality" who would
go on national TV and confess to a series of killings,
as happened in this drama. That is not the way it
works. If a personality would consider violence, the
other personalities would try to stop it. Healthier parts
would probably rotate out to prevent such plans. Despite experiencing violence, most dissociators go over-

board to prevent violence, and they certainly go over-board to avoid public humiliation. The thought of a public confession would scramble the whole system, to the point where the person would, no doubt, be speechless in front of the cameras. Protective person-alities would act to stop a public confession.

The writers of that TV movie have no idea how far they were from the truth about multiples being dan-gerous. One of my clients read an earlier draft of this chapter and reminded me of something she had told me a few weeks ago, which supports this point. Dur-ing her teen years, when her most rebellious person-ality was in charge much of the time, that personality had a perfect chance to get the ultimate revenge on a person who had abused her. She happened to be at home when he had a heart attack, and stopped breathing. Other family members did nothing. The re-action of this teen part was, at first, glee—she could let him die, and would not have to be on-guard about being abused by him anymore. But, as he laid there, she decided to come to the man's rescue. She gave him mouth-to-mouth, which kept him alive until the arrival of an ambulance. Talk about drama! That is the kind of TV show we would be seeing if we had documentaries instead of entertainment. This woman values life—even the life of her abuser—more than she values her own safety. When the personality most capable of being vengeful had a chance to let the man die, the system chose life. That is the truth about danger and dissociation.

If there are exceptions to that rule, it is very impor-tant to emphasize that they are exceptions. The rule is this: Dissociators value life. They are not danger-ous. You do not have to wonder if they are secretly carrying a knife under their coat. TV writers need to tell the truth about this because failure to do so un-fairly stigmatizes brave and innocent individuals.

A Profile

Do you want to know what dissociative people look like? They look like everybody else most of the time. They blend in with those around them, except in their areas of talent, where they excel. One thing which seems clear to me is they avoid drastic behaviors. Internal balance is a skill they live by, because they have a drive to live a healthy life. They get along well with most people, excel in some areas, and avoid the spotlight in situations where they may look bad.

Here is a real life example. To the outside world, Gina could easily be seen as a model person. A worship leader and a gifted musician, she contributes regularly to the spiritual life of her church. She is a school teacher, and the parents of her students can hardly say enough good things about her. However, during the past few years, the problems she had been able to keep undercover have led her to therapy for dissociation. While therapy is underway she is doing her best to keep her life in its rhythm, doing the things she does well, and receiving healing for memories that used to be dissociated.

As is the case for practically all my clients, the last thing Gina wants is the public label, multiple personality disorder. What a mistake it would be to jeopardize her teaching position by announcing she is a multiple. Stereotypical thinking is just too strong among her acquaintances. Those people would not understand.

Last week Gina asked me what to tell her nine-year-old daughter, who said something which indicated she knows Gina is a multiple. Gina and her husband, who is her therapy partner, thought it could be a mistake to let the child know she is correct. There is the problem of whether she could understand that MPD is not an illness, and there is the problem of what to do if the daughter tells somebody about the MPD and it becomes public knowledge. Gina and her husband told me they do not want to lie to their daughter, but since false stereotypes about multiplicity are so pervasive, they are stumped.

I told them to tell the daughter she is right about her observations. But, because MPD is not understood by the public very well, I said to tell her it would not be a good idea for other people to know. I said to mention it is God's gift which is helping you recover from an awful childhood.

"Please say it helps you do all the things you do. You are a very good musician and a very good teacher," I said, "and do not forget to tell her you are also a loving mother. Your 'mother part' has been able to give her so much love because dissociation has protected your love from negative childhood feelings. Tell her dissociation makes it easier for you to love."

CHAPTER 5:

Anything overwhelming can be dissociated. Events which involve shock, terror, physical abuse, and sexual abuse, are often dissociated and lead to multiple personality disorder/dissociative identity disorder.

What Is Ritual Abuse?

Ritual Abuse (RA) involves all of the above, and therefore, usually causes dissociation. Nobody knows what percentage of people who dissociate have been through RA. Estimates have ranged from 10 percent to 70 percent, and I figure it must be somewhere in the neighborhood of 50 percent overall, but percentages may vary from place to place, depending on concentrations of active ritual groups.

When a client dissociates, the therapist usually has no clues about what led to the original split. The clues which indicate RA sometimes do not emerge early in treatment, and may appear for the first time much later. This makes it difficult to estimate the incidence of RA. If someone has MPD/DID, that alone certainly does not suggest that RA was part of the person's past. The memories which come up will indicate RA, but until the memories emerge, therapists have no reason to expect it may be part of a person's history.

RA is so terrifying and painful that dissociation almost always results. Dissociation is about the only way a child can respond to that degree of disruption.

One therapy group works intensively with survivors for a week or two, and returns them to their primary therapist to resume therapy. They have found that of the approximately ninety RA survivors they have treated, only one or two have not dissociated the RA memories. It appears that although dissociation does not indicate RA, RA almost always indicates dissociation. RA is so overwhelming, the mind needs to split off from the event in order to maintain proper functioning.

Therapy plans for people who dissociate—MPD/DID—usually include these three target areas: (1) creating a healthy living environment, (2) promoting cooperation among personality parts, and (3) healing memories. If RA comes up, those three treatment areas remain the targets of therapy. Usually, the person's behaviors indicate dissociation before the cause is known. The treatment framework for RA is not different than for other dissociative conditions, just targeted to the unique needs of the individual.

People use different terms for various kinds of RA. I believe "Ritual Abuse" is the term heard most often. It seems to be accepted as the main heading over other subheadings, which describe different types of RA. Here are the most commonly used terms, and explanations of how they describe different kinds of abuse.

Ritualistic Abuse

Ritual is defined as a religious ceremony. It is a rite, or an act of worship which is to be carried out in a prescribed way. Clearly, *ritual* is a religious term. However, the adverb *ritualistic* does not necessarily imply something religious, and can be used in a broader sense. It can mean any activity which is carried out in a predictable way on a certain occasion. Let me offer two examples of abuse situations which could be understood as ritualistic, in the broader sense.

Michael was awakened as a child each morning by a mother who followed a predictable pattern. She would walk down the hallway, her shoes hitting the floor hard enough to wake him up. Next, she would open his door and call him names. That was ritualistic abuse, in that it was an activity he could count on to happen the same way, at the same time, in the same place, each day.

He dreaded it. He knew he would wake up to shame each day. His feelings would be strongly negative, knowing it would happen each morning. His identity was damaged by the mother's ritual. He came to believe what she said about him was true. Memories about the mother's ritualistic behavior were repressed. (The morning events were not shocking enough to cause him to dissociate, and his knowledge of the repressed events came back gradually.) When Michael sought therapy, it was for self-image issues.

The morning ritual became an issue for Michael after he had been in therapy for a few months. He knew the repressed ritual was true. He sort of remembered it, but he had needed to forget it, in order to get on with his adult life. He knew he was more valuable than his mother said he was each morning, and validation of that point in therapy helped him immensely.

Teresa's ritualistic memories were dissociated. There was something about her relationships with men that did not work for her. She became highly agitated when things started to get sexual; she became obedient, and she could not stop becoming involved. She also became nervous near the end of Sunday morning worship services.

The abusive pattern which became uncovered during therapy was ritualistic in this way: Her father was a pastor, and many Sunday afternoons he would take his little girl, Teresa, on an automobile ride for some "father and daughter time." As we talked about the rides, she started to sense the same agitation that came up around sexual issues. The father led her into a sexual relationship during those Sunday afternoon drives, and it had an effect which was quite similar to other ritualistic abuse cases I have seen.

When she was still a child, she would get anxious as the Sunday morning service ended, anticipating the afternoon car ride with her father. The abuse events were dissociated in midchildhood, but they interfered with her adult life in church, and when she became attracted to men. Those instances of conscious interference became predictable, which is expected in ritualistic abuse. Whenever the ritualistic pattern begins—sitting in a church service, or being attracted to somebody—the abuse is expected to follow.

When the memory of her father's abuse emerged in therapy, it did not seem to Teresa as though it could have happened to her, and she had great difficulty accepting it. It helped her to accept the truth about the memory when she learned that her father had been charged by his denomination for alleged sexual improprieties with a girl in his youth group. All this was very upsetting—the memories of her own abuse, and discovering that her father had probably molested others—but it was what she had to face in order to prepare for improved relationships with men.

The term *ritualistic abuse* applies correctly to many situations. The effect of rituals is mind control. Rituals train people to respond in a specific way, and to hold false beliefs. Teresa acted obediently when older men became sexual with her. Michael believed every negative word his mother said to him. Rituals usually include a strong fear response, and it is hard to break their controlling effect.

Sadistic Ritual Abuse

The first word of this term indicates sexual perversion. *Sadistic* derives from the writings of the marquis de Sade, whose works contain descriptions of sexual perversions. Sadistic Ritual Abuse describes what has happened to clients who have survived grotesquely perverse ritualistic abuse. If, for example, Michael's mother had been perversely sexual each morning, Sadistic Ritual Abuse would be the correct term to describe her behavior.

Satanic Ritual Abuse

I believe this is the term to use when abuse is carried out in satanic worship, where rites—illegal acts—are carried out by secret covens. The Church of Satan says it practices nothing illegal, so this does not refer to worshipping in the Church of Satan. Satanic Ritual Abuse (SRA) refers to rituals which usually include animal or human sacrifice, and perverse forms of sexual abuse, performed privately.

Knowledge about SRA comes from those who have been there and survived—they escaped. Coven members who remain active will not disclose anything because they would immediately be landed in jail or be killed by fellow members. Rituals would not continue if discovered because they are illegal. Survivor accounts are consistent across the country, around the world, and over the course of history. This is not new and it is not local.[1]

Perhaps the most concise definition comes from the report of the Ritual Abuse Task Force, Los Angeles County Commission for Women:

> Ritual abuse is a brutal form of abuse of children, adolescents, and adults, consisting of physical, sexual, and psychological abuse, and involving the use of rituals. Ritual does not nec-

essarily mean satanic. However, most survivors state that they were ritually abused as part of satanic worship for the purpose of indoctrinating them into satanic beliefs and practices. Ritual abuse rarely consists of a single episode. It usually involves repeated abuse over an extended period of time.

The physical abuse is severe, sometimes including torture and killing. The sexual abuse is usually painful, sadistic, and humiliating, intended as a means of gaining dominance over the victim. The psychological abuse is devastating and involves the use of ritual/indoctrination, which includes mind control techniques and mind altering drugs, and ritual/intimidation which conveys to the victim a profound terror of the cult members and of the evil spirits they believe cult members can command. Both during and after the abuse, most victims are in a state of terror, mind control, and dissociation in which disclosure is exceedingly difficult.[2]

World Views and Religion

I believe it is more acceptable in the 1990s to talk about the spiritual dimensions of life than it has been for a long time. A Gallup poll found that 90 percent of adults in America pray. Another Gallup poll found that 74 percent of adults believe Jesus is the way to eternal life. Those numbers are surprising, considering the content of America's textbooks. The official educational point of view in America is that religious people are a minority. But, Gallup pollsters are finding that atheists and agnostics are the minority. The notion that something evolved out of nothing and turned into life, has not gathered much momentum. It looks like people have little confidence in science as a guide to finding meaning in life. The majority still seek meaning through religious commitment. Our educational system should put the Gallup poll findings in our children's texts. The majority of people in our country still consider this to be a nation "under God."

A person's world view is a powerful force in determining behavior and thought. Religious practices are based on a religion's world view, which could fall into one of two categories—monistic or dualistic. SRA needs to be understood as a religion with a dualistic world view, as we will soon see.

Monism is a term used to describe the world view of any religion which teaches that all spirits are good. Native religions are usually monistic, as are many contemporary religions. One radio host asked me about exorcism, and in my answer I used the term *evil spirit*. He lectured me about looking for some good in any spirit being. He is New Age, which is monistic. In monistic rites, people open themselves up to whatever spirits may be present.

Christianity maintains a "dualistic" world view. It teaches that spirits may be evil or good, and spirits' actions are determined by their leader—the Almighty God or Satan. It is believed Satan led a rebellious horde of angels away from God, and this horde intends to destroy God's creation and unseat God from His throne.

Here is the way most Christians view the struggle on earth. Citizens in the Kingdom of God spread the good news and train disciples everywhere they go, empowered by the Holy Spirit. Whenever they do that, they get resistance from Satan, his evil spirits, and from people whose allegiance is to Satan.

Worship and Rituals

It is hard to grasp what could cause people to carry out the unspeakable acts commonly attributed to SRA perpetrators. People come up with different conclusions. Some write it off—they honestly believe that the SRA accounts are the product of hysterical imaginations. That point of view has a time-honored tradition—Dr. Freud's. Others believe SRA might happen occasionally, but is not widespread. The point of view that makes sense to me is expressed in the final paragraph of an article in the *Journal of Psychology and Theology*: "There is no longer room for denial and disbelief—for evading the grim reality of SRA. . . . Solid scientific inquiry does not allow us that luxury; neither should Christian conscience."[3]

I understand why people participate in SRA. It is a religion with a dualistic world view—it is worshipping evil, and working against everything that is good. Not only are SRA perpetrators active during worship rites— their lives reflect the evil of their lord, Satan. Evil acts are carried out to prove allegiance to Satan. This recognition seems to be missing when most people try to explain SRA.

When Christians go to church they worship together. They call on God to empower them with His Spirit so they will have strength to do His work in the world. Singing and praising Him together, the spiritual lift is "a touch of heaven." God's presence is tangibly there, and the reality of His goodness is inescapable.

From what survivors tell me, the opposite goes on in satanic rituals. Satan is worshipped, and his followers call on him to fill them with evil spirits, so they can do his work in the world. They do things to prove their allegiance—illegal things—the things survivors would like to forget, but cannot. Chanting together and calling him their lord, the rituals are described as extremely oppressive. An evil presence is profoundly there, it is unforgettable, and it is difficult to explain to those of us who have not been there.

I remember an account of what Pres. Sadaam Hussein did to gain control over his cabinet, shortly after his party came to power in Iraq. A newspaper reported that a cabinet minister disagreed with him about a certain policy. Hussein responded by giving the other cabinet members automatic weapons, took them all outside, and ordered them to execute the dissenter, which they did! Despite the fact that they had no choice but to obey, two lies will follow those cabinet members for the rest of their lives: They are guilty of killing the man who disagreed with their leader, and they are evil because of what they did.

The parallels between the actions of Sadaam Hussein in this account, and the things survivors say about SRA perpetrators are remarkable. Little children are forced to kill, and then told they are forever guilty and evil. What difficult lies to break. Mind control is what Hussein and the SRA perpetrators practice, and they are very good at it.

As the L.A. County Commission for Women has put it, many perpetrators of RA worship Satan. They indoctrinate those who are forced to participate, into satanic beliefs and practices. This is religious training. In their religion, those who contradict the leader may not see the dawn. They must obey and do the things which force them to falsely conclude that they will be forever guilty and evil.

A client recently brought me a magazine article which showed some pictures of the Switzerland mass cult killing. One scene showed a basement in a building which belonged to that group. The basement's floor was bright red with a gold pentagram outlined in the middle, an altar was in the center of the pentagram, and candles were strewn all over the room. The article talked about the mass murder of the cult members, but did not talk about worship. That does not surprise me. In editing the story, the magazine chose to completely ignore the obvious visual evidence of worship. But, the reader can deduce what happened:

A lot of deaths, a pentagram, and other worship items in a basement, where things can happen which nobody from the outside world will be able to see—unmistakably, SRA. That is one instance where the obvious facts which should lead to the uncovering of SRA were ignored. How many other instances have there been?

Christians would point out what Jesus said: "There is nothing concealed that will not be disclosed, or hidden that will not be made known. What you have said in the dark will be heard in the daylight, and what you have whispered in the ear in the inner rooms will be proclaimed from the roofs" (Luke 12:2-3). The basement picture proclaims a thousand words from the roofs—Satanic Ritual Abuse. The truth has been proclaimed. Nothing stays hidden. Sooner or later, the truth surfaces.

CHAPTER 6:

What the Accusers Do Not Say

Why Do Some People Deny Their Memories Are True?

Perhaps the most convincing argument that there is such a thing as a false memory is when someone publicly accuses a former therapist of creating the memories. What a powerful accusation that is! Radio, TV, and tabloids compete for that kind of story. It gets top priority. The client seems honest enough, displays the correct feelings, and is asked questions which lead to the conclusion that the therapist is at fault. The former client is the victim and the therapist is the bad guy. The story appears irrefutable.

How hard it is for the listener to gather all the facts. That kind of story is not a documentary, and should not be presented as though it were. It is one person's perspective, and the interviewer usually does not dig deep enough to get all the facts. The spin on the story makes it seem like this is a precedent-setting situation, and must be merely the tip of an iceberg. Listeners are called on by the former client to punish therapists who drag nice people into the pit of hell, and break the hearts of their families. But, there is more to the picture.

Here are three things the accusers do not say, which the interviewers do not ask, but which certainly belong in the picture.

Only a Small Percentage of Clients with Memories of Extreme Abuse Blame Their Therapists

The number of accusations by clients who could blame their therapists for memories of abuse is well under 1 percent.[1] Anybody who knows statistical theory will tell you what that means: It means the claims of the very few are not likely representative. If there were any sort of a trend, we would be seeing a lot of accusations. However, what we are seeing is that the vast majority of clients are sticking with their therapy, and growing healthier. The majority of clients are doing better, and that is what good documentation would discover. That is missing in this picture.

The Accusations Lack Specificity

Accusing former clients believe their therapists must have said something misleading, but exactly what, where, and when is missing. If the therapists were using mind control tactics, memories of therapist abuse would be coming up, in the same way memories of ritual abuse come up. Since specific memories of mind control manipulations supposedly carried out by therapists are not surfacing in peoples' minds, and specific mind control memories of abuse are, we should be getting different conclusions than those made by accusers. We have many documented specific memories of extreme abuse (see appendix A), so in the absence of specific memories of therapist abuse, the guilty finger should be pointing in another direction.

Clients Who Have Renounced Their Memories May Not Be Getting the Truth from Family Members

Researchers, talk show producers, and journalists really need to check out the accusers' charges. I know of many examples of misleading accusations which have been incorrectly accepted as the truth. That is another missing part of the picture portrayed in false memory stories.

In a letter to the state licensing board for psychologists, the father of an adult client accused an intern at my clinic of using mind control, of splitting up their family, etc. That occurred a few years ago, before anyone had heard of the term *false memory syndrome*, but the charges were the same as those raised today by family members who accuse therapists. This father charged that I had misdiagnosed his daughter, and drafted a letter charging me with three pages of offenses. To look at the letter, it would appear this man enlisted a good detective agency, and built a very strong case against me.

One of the charges stated I had referred a few patients to a particular hospital with the diagnosis of MPD, and it was stated that the hospital staff found my diagnoses were incorrect. Since no client's names were mentioned in the letter, it appeared this father's accusations may be true. Two weaknesses in this charge immediately come to mind. (1) Confidentiality of client records is required by law. There is no way he would have the knowledge to make that charge. He would not have access to his daughter's files at our clinic, nor would he have access to hospital files to find other diagnoses. It is practically impossible that the father could have obtained the confidential information needed to document this claim. (2) At that time I had never hospitalized any of my clients for any reason! The accusations could not possibly be true, and, most assuredly, the father knew they were untrue. He had to be confabulating the so-called evidence behind this charge, and was fully aware he was doing so.

The father's letter also included the names of some therapists, whom he said he had contacted, and each is supposed to have told him they believe I am wrong in my approach to therapy. I know one of the therapists he listed, so I called him up. He said this father had indeed telephoned him about me, but the therapist had said very complimentary things about me. He told the father he has worked with MPD and SRA, he has heard me present seminars for therapists, and he agrees completely with my approach.

That father must think I do not do my homework if he is going to put my supporters on his list of accusers. The three pages of charges were not supported by the evidence he gave. However, if his daughter read that dishonest letter about me without verifying the evidence, she may have joined the father in accusing the intern and me of malpractice. It was a very powerfully worded letter, and it could have easily disengaged her from therapy.

Anyone can write accusatory letters about therapists, but if they claim to represent a large number of misdiagnosed clients, if they lack specificity, and if their accounts are not verified, they must be viewed as tainted, and maybe even confabulated. As I understand things, therapists are not the only ones who will be sued over the false memory issue—so will false accusers. Making up lies about a therapist is slander.

The Majority of Therapists—by a Huge Margin—Believe Clients' Accounts of Ritual Abuse

The only data I have which shed light on this topic, come from a study I participated in. Questionnaires were sent to therapists—psychiatrists, psychologists, social workers, and other disciplines—to discover the effects on therapists of working with dissociative patients.[2] The respondents are not beginners—most have over twelve years of clinical practice, and have seen between six and twenty dissociative clients. These are licensed or certified professionals, so we expect they are a well-trained, scientifically astute group. Of the 1185 respondents, 88 percent reported belief in ritual abuse, only 4 percent disbelieved, and the other 8 percent reported neutrality. Here is how I understand those numbers: Experienced professionals believe by a huge margin—88 percent to 4 percent (22 to 1!)—that ritual abuse is real. I wonder why that study is not mentioned by reporters.

Things Which Lead to Denial That Memories Are True

Personality Parts Do Not Know What Each Other Have Said

One client who was pretty far along in her progress told me something which happened early in treatment with another therapist. As she explained it, one of her parts was sexualized by her father and told the therapist about the incest. It was a dissociated memory and apparently, after the conclusion of that therapy session, her host part did not remember anything the sexualized part had shared. During a subsequent session the therapist started talking about the reported incest and the host immediately responded, "I never said my father did that to me."

I can imagine the therapist was at a loss to explain to the host exactly what had happened. The host part of her system wanted, more than anything in the world, to maintain good relations with her family. The host had only experienced good things from the father. Incest had taken place during the night, so the dissociated part was the only one who knew about that aspect of her father's attention. The other parts sensed he was good to her, and even preferred her to the other children. Over time, the truth about the father's nighttime behavior spread to the other parts, and the host came to accept what the sexualized part was saying about the father. But, at the moment the host first heard the therapist say something about incest, her life could easily have gone in another direction. She could have claimed the therapist was implanting false ideas, since she did not know what the sexualized part had said. The information was new to the host, and it was a shock. If she had gone to court to disallow what the other part of her had said, she would have been a hero to those who believe therapists are the bad guys.

Feelings Get Too Intense

It is very difficult to get in touch with memories when they carry strong feelings. In fact, dealing with intense feelings is exactly what dissociation helps people do. It keeps people distant from difficult feelings. One of my clients got in touch with a memory of SRA, and the jolting effect on her host had to be resolved. Either she was going to deny any of it was true, or she was going to have to let her host get in touch with the intense SRA feelings. At first, she tried to deny everything, but her SRA-abused parts would not let her. With encouragement from a friend, the host learned to deal with the very difficult feelings.

However, this could have been another chance for a false memory charge. It would have been understandable if she had stayed in denial of what the ritually abused parts were sharing with the host. She tried to find other ways to explain what her mind was telling her, but in the long run her dissociated parts would not be ignored. The false memory cause lost that battle, and she continued to pursue health.

Renewed Abuse Can Reverse Progress

There are a number of cases I have heard about which fall into this category. After therapy is well underway, the person gets reabused by the original perpetrator, and therapy changes direction. Sometimes the new direction is to go ahead and finally accuse the perpetrator, but sometimes the new direction is to accuse the therapist of making everything up!

A 1988 article illustrates how deceptive and malicious perpetrators can be, if they fear their deeds may be exposed. This article was written before the term *false memory syndrome* had been manufactured. I find it interesting to see how the therapist tried to withstand pressure from a perpetrator who claimed he was victimized by false memories, before such a term could be used in his defense:

> Early in the therapy of a patient with suspected multiple personality disorder, a therapist began hearing about vague memories of physical and sexual abuse in childhood. Angry and tearful personalities appeared and began relating details of the abuse which was reported to have been sadistic and persisted over years. . . . [The therapist] interviewed the patient's father, the alleged abuser and a respected minister . . . , who emphatically denied any abuse, and informed the therapist that the patient was a liar even as a child. In a subsequent discussion . . . the patient stated that she had lied about the abuse to get attention from the therapist and had faked multiple personalities. She proceeded to talk about her father's good qualities as a minister and parent, and was remorseful about maligning such an innocent person. The therapist, feeling vastly relieved of the burden of pur-

suing the issue of abuse any further, talked with
the patient about the necessity of getting attention for positive actions rather than through false
accusations. The patient was subsequently not
prepared for a visit home to her father where
she was attacked and raped, which was confirmed by medical examination.[3]

Evidently, the patient did expose the actions of the
father, but it could have gone the other way. The renewed abuse could easily have ended therapy, and
the father could have sued the therapist. I know of a
case where that happened.

The therapist told me a client had been making
good progress, but had gone out of town to visit her
parents for a holiday. When she returned, the therapist had no idea who this person was! A personality
she had never met came into the office and accused
her of creating false memories. It looked like she was
abused again during her trip home, and her system of
personalities was completely rearranged by the time
she came back.

The case was still in court as I wrote this. Even if
the therapist was acquitted, as she should be, she
suffered a great deal from the adverse, untrue publicity. She also suffered from the tremendous burden
she carried while preparing for the trial. For a while,
she was fighting depression because of the false
memory accusations, and was strapped financially due
to court costs and job-related repercussions. Even
though she is doing better now, she is a victim. We
need to ask ourselves if she should be found guilty of
listening to a client's personal history. That is not an
accusation which should stick. But, taking into account
how convincing the client's accusing personality can
be and how powerful the family is, the case is already
a defeat for the therapist. It has been trial by headline.
The half-truths and outright lies carried by the press
have been terribly damaging.

Figure 3 illustrates two ways personality systems can change. In these cases, when the truth becomes known, the therapist is not found to be the perpetrator. The abuse happened elsewhere. The whole truth needs to be known, including both the past and present, if the accusations are to be properly considered.

Anyone Can Be Mistakenly Accused

My heart is deeply touched by the predicament of well-meaning family members who honestly believe they have no options but to expose the therapist allegedly responsible for producing false memories in their loved one. They resort to threatening legal action and sending intimidating letters to the therapist. Here are two such letters I received since the first draft of this chapter.

It is interesting to note they are the only letters of this variety I have received to date. They arrived within a few days of one another, and carry the same message—both conclude I am a religious nut, and suggest I am about to be sued for malpractice. I have never met these people. Neither letter is signed and both are sent to the same California address. Typed and lacking any identifying information, they were sent from cities in Texas and Maryland. I have no idea who could have sent them.

The first one is postmarked 12 December 1994:

Dr. James Friesen:

I am writing you because you need to know the impact and destructive results of your misguided family therapy practice. Our family has been destroyed by your therapy, which was based on assumed satanic ritual abuse in early childhood because of your multiple personality disorder misdiagnosis. No attempt was made to contact us nor to validate the repressed memories.

FEELINGS GET TOO INTENSE

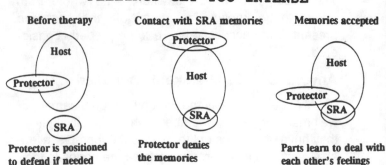

RENEWED ABUSE REVERSES PROGRESS

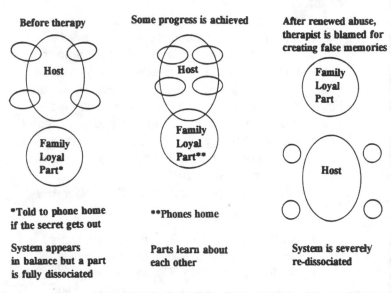

Figure 3: CHANGES WHICH CAN LEAD TO DENIAL

To treat for repressed memories without any effort at external validation is malpractice pure and simple. Malpractice on the basis of standards of care that have developed out of the history of psychiatric service—as with witches—and malpractice because a misdirection of therapy has caused irreparable injuries to your patient and our family.

Your pursuit of Satan has been very fruitful and he has consumed you and your zealous cultlike practice. How dare you determine an MPD diagnosis caused by SRA with no face to face encounter with the alleged perpetrators and with no external validation.

During this happy and joyous time of year, I pray for the Lord's mercy on your soul for the many families, including ours, that have been ripped asunder by your continuing malpractice.

A still grieving family

[No signature]

The second letter is postmarked 15 December 1994:

James Friesen,

It is my utmost prayer each night that the devastation and destruction you have wrought on innocent families will be returned to you tenfold. You must get vicarious pleasures out of consorting with Satan. Unfortunately, you have drawn a member of my family into your insanity, destroying what was once a happy family with your innuendo, suggestion, and implanting of false memories that never happened.

May God have mercy on your soul for the evil you have done to innocent people. The Satan which you seek has surely found you, and hopefully will destroy your greedy, money grubbing business that you created for nothing but fame, power, and glory, in order to place yourself above the families you have destroyed. Fortunately, more and more psych "mills" such as yours are being driven out of business. But that will not bring my adult child back from the dead where you have placed your victims. You should be incarcerated in a mental institution before you do more damage to mankind.

When evil ones such as you die, there is rejoicing in heaven. May the evil you have done be returned to you tenfold.

A parent whose loving family you destroyed.

It appears the writers have come under the influence of groups who blame therapists for creating false memories. Certain words and phrases show up which reflect stances taken by false memory-fighting groups. Both writers have certainly been coached somewhere about writing letters to therapists, and the dates on the letters suggest the writers may have heard "how to do it" from the same source. Both letters avoid leaving the slightest traceable evidence as to who the senders are—letters and envelopes were typed, and nothing was handwritten.

"Innuendo, suggestion, and implanting of false memories"; "repressed memories without any effort at external validation"; "malpractice on the basis of standards of care"; "misdirection of therapy"; and "psych 'mills' such as yours" are phrases routinely used by such groups. And what a pity. Instead of aiding the recovery of beloved family members while they are in therapy, energy is spent writing letters to divert them from receiving the help they need.

Terms like *malpractice*, *misdiagnosis*, *standards of care*, and *driven out of business* clearly are intended to alert me that lawsuits are not far away. I have been told that groups opposed to false memory predict we will soon see many, many cases in court, with countless victims of "repressed memory therapy" successfully exposing incompetent therapists. Although nobody knows at this point how many charges are being made by former clients, we know many families of former clients who are bringing charges against therapists. However, in most cases the charges are dropped. Licensing boards and judges usually see the deceptive nature of the charges, and the cases go nowhere. The truth is that these family members have no direct evidence whatsoever about malpractice. Their cases are based entirely on innuendo, suggestion, and false charges.

It surprises me that those letters contend I am a destructive, cultlike religious fanatic, involved in the pursuit of Satan and of power. I do not think about Satan very much at all. I am a mainstream Christian and base my life on teachings like this New Testament passage.

> Do not let any unwholesome talk come out of your mouths, but only what is helpful for building others up according to their needs, that it may benefit those who listen. . . . Get rid of all bitterness, rage and anger, brawling and slander, along with every form of malice. Be kind and compassionate to one another, forgiving each other, just as in Christ God forgave you. Be imitators of God, therefore, as dearly loved children and live a life of love, just as Christ loved us. (Eph. 4:29–5:2)

If therapy in my office were destructive, as the letters contend, I would be out of business. People would quit coming. There is no way my outpatient practice could be cultlike because clients only see me one or two hours weekly, and are asked to bring therapy partners to every session. There is no secret about what happens in my office: Clients improve their living skills, address psychological and spiritual conflicts in a supportive environment, and family and friends support recovery through involvement in therapy, if they are invited by the client. Clients are free to stop coming at any time, and they are free to avoid contact with any people who seem unsafe to them. If something cultlike were going on in my office, they would object, and so would their partners.

To the charge I am in pursuit of power over the minds of clients, I can only say that is the opposite of what I seek. Everything I do is designed to empower them! My therapeutic objectives and goals always maintain that perspective. Those who have been abused experience profound powerlessness as a result. My greatest pleasure as a therapist comes when they develop their internal power enough to be in control of their own lives. From my earliest contact with clients, I encourage them to develop confidence in their abilities, to protect themselves, and to pursue maturity. If the "grieving parents" would get acquainted with my writings and my seminar presentations, they would find that the development of power in the client is what I seek.

I do not believe the parents who wrote those letters are sources of evil, even though it appears they think I am. Evil probably struck when their children were abused, and the ripples have not yet stopped spreading. By believing the lies of groups who pretend extreme child abuse is rare, they too have been affected by the ripples of evil. Regretfully, they add to the suffering when they seek to cover up the truth about child abuse. That does not work. In the end, nothing remains hidden. May God help us all as we face the awful truth about the evil things some people do to other people.

Evil Happens, but So Does Good

When evil happens, it spreads. The ripple effect takes place all the time. That is the way evil is. It contaminates and has a tendency to keep on contaminating.

After spending thousands of hours with survivors of extreme abuse, I have seen how evil can spread. For example, here is how pedophilia spreads. Pedophiles apparently average at least fifty child victims during the course of their lifetimes![4] That is horrible, but that is not where it stops. Perhaps 10 percent of those child victims are damaged enough to become pedophiles themselves, so the next generation (5 pedophiles) averages 250 victims (50 per offender), and the generation after that (25 pedophiles) averages 1250 victims! These are the kinds of math calculations we need, in order to show how there can be so many people reporting they have been abused. Perhaps it will help people believe what researchers are telling us—about one-third of the population has suffered some form of child abuse. Evil happens.

But I do not dwell on evil in therapy. The people I work with—clients, their therapy partners, and my fellow therapists—concentrate on living. We set living a productive life as the top priority. Dealing with the effects of evil is secondary to that goal. People do not want to remain subject to terror and fear, so the evil events they have survived need to be handled as part of treatment. Perhaps the most crucial aspect of therapy is activating clients' natural abilities and helping them remain productive, so they can keep on doing the things that bring them satisfaction. If clients can live most of the time in their healthy parts, the wounded parts—those stuck by evil—benefit from the enriching living environment.

Many times therapy does not take people along an easy path. On the way they receive some outside help which is more than simply coincidental, and it has a wonderful effect. Good happens.

As the huge blizzard was about to hit the coast of Massachusetts in March of 1993, I was flying into Boston's Logan airport. On the escalator going down to collect my baggage, I heard my name on the loud-speakers. "Dr. James Friesen, will you . . . ," but the rest of the message faded because I was at a point exactly between two floors. At the bottom of the esca-lator, I went to the information booth, but could not find out what the message was. I stuck around a bit, collected my baggage, and eventually went back up to an airline counter to ask if they knew where I could get the message. The delays continued for at least ten minutes.

The message was to meet the person who would pick me up near the top of the escalator! If the mes-sage had been announced a few seconds earlier, I would have met that person, and we would have been off without delay. There would have been no ten-minute wait. That was not merely happenstance. During that wait, a pilot who was reading my second book in the pilots' lounge heard the message on the loudspeaker, and went to meet me at the top of the escalator. His wife was hospitalized with MPD, and reading my books was his assignment so he would be able to under-stand her better.

By the time I got to the escalator, he was talking with the man who would give me a ride. He introduced himself, and asked if I was the author of the book he was holding. When I said yes, he told me he needed to find a therapist in his Midwest town for his wife after she got out of the hospital, and did I know any good therapists there? As chance would have it, I did. I got out my address book, gave him the therapist's name and telephone number, and we spoke about his wife for another five minutes or so. The man who picked me up had been talking with the captain while they were waiting. He said the captain told him he is not a spiritual type of person, but since his wife was, he read my material, which includes both psychological and spiritual aspects of therapy.

Most of the time when incidents like this happen I never find how things turn out. A few months later I met the therapist who worked with the captain's wife when she was hospitalized and asked if he remembered them. A broad smile came across his face. He said that following our conversation at the airport, the captain was a changed man. The captain had said, "God did something for me."

He had previously been a questioning sort of spouse, second-guessing, trying to understand, but generally not helping his wife's progress very much. Now he was a model husband of an SRA survivor. He made frequent visits while his wife was still hospitalized, and his attitude was tremendously uplifting for her. He told her therapist he believes it was no coincidence my name was on the loudspeaker at the right moment, which gave him enough time to meet me, and get the local therapist's name.

The wife had taken the name and phone number I had given to the captain and was now in therapy with that therapist. She seemed to be doing fairly well. This was not coincidental. The captain was now more supportive of his wife. Whatever cult abuse had happened to her was real. But in the end, supportive people were brought together in just the right way to assist her through recovery. God did something for her. Good does happen.

In my lifetime I may help fifty people improve the quality of their lives. Perhaps 10 percent of them will help others, but maybe it will be more than 10 percent—maybe 20 percent or higher. I believe good can be expected to spread faster than evil. If 20 percent of those who receive help in my office begin to help others, the next generation receiving help would be five hundred, and if 20 percent of those are positive influences in peoples' lives, five thousand people will be better off in the following generation! Good has a ripple effect too.

When people are in the middle of pain in my office, it is hard for me to see anything good coming from the work they are doing. Tears, terror, and anxiety—that is the way many sessions go. Even if those sessions end on a positive note, people who open up about pain in their lives get exhausted. Periods may go by—weeks or months—in which progress does not seem to be taking place. Depression, hopelessness, and suicidal thoughts need to be worked through. I am often unaware they are making steady progress.

Looking back over the past few years, I can see that good is being spread because of them. They are already making a difference. Twenty five or fifty years from now, many thousands of people who would otherwise continue in their suffering may find that supportive people come together in just the right way to assist them in recovery, because of the work being done today.

Those who have suffered the most seem ready and able to help the most. What a discovery that has been. Even though survivors of extreme abuse are reluctant to share their very personal struggles in public, they are not reluctant at all to help others.

Reporters from major TV networks and some independent researchers included me in their quest for the right story about trauma survivors. They started out telling me they wanted to spend some time with a survivor of extreme abuse, so they could produce a good documentary. As we got further into our conversations, it became evident they were really looking for cases that are going to court—stories about innocent people who have had terrible things happen to them, where the bad guy goes to prison. When I told reporters I don't know anyone who is going to court, they quickly lost interest. If they want a documentary which reflects what is really going on, they should look for people who are not going to court. The majority want to stay out of court. A good documentary may not find traceable evidence of terrible things, and may not end up with a convicted perpetrator, but would probably show survivors of extreme abuse creating worthwhile lives for themselves, despite the terrible things that happened to them.

Preparing to Read Part II

The next part of this book is a documentary about three dissociative clients from my caseload, SRA survivors, and about their therapy partners. The chapters are transcriptions of taped discussions I had with them. As the reader will see, their privacy needs to be protected. They would prefer to avoid the controversy which would result from going public. However, I am convinced that without their input, the reader will find this book to be little more than an intellectual exercise. Part II brings color to the picture. It is more than a footnote which supports Part I. It is people talking about life and about living—people whose stories need to be included in the endeavor to understand recovered memories.

Those who see me in therapy are usually Christians, which is understandable because I work in a Christian counseling center. Dividing the material into topic headings for Part II has not been easy, because the topics flow together and resist separation. Spiritual material is interspersed among the other topics because spirituality intermingles with other aspects of patients' lives. God is in the middle of everything we do together, so it is hard to separate the spiritual from the psychological dimensions of therapy.

As you read the conversations with survivors and their partners, try to see things through their eyes, even though it will not be easy to understand their experiences fully. Despite the many hours I have spent with them, I must admit my understanding is still limited. It is hard to know what their traumas were like because we were not there, so our empathy will necessarily be restricted. But, as you read the accounts, you may become able to be supportive to a similar individual some day, which may be exactly what is needed.

The recovery of memories which are terrifying life-events leaves an indelible effect on people, and it changes those with whom they share the experience. Prepare to change as you get to know these people and what they have been through. Expect to increase your knowledge about what life is like with the wrong diagnosis, flashbacks, what "memory work" is like, how the false memory controversy affects those in therapy, what it is like to discover ritual abuse memories, and what it is like to be a therapy partner for a survivor of extreme abuse.

The truth about traumatic memories must include the truth about surviving the traumas, living with their effects, and recovering from them. Looking for truthful understanding of memories is not separate from looking at the person's whole life. What effects suggest a traumatic cause? How is the survivor doing? What does her future look like? Does her life have integrity? Can we see how the traumas have influenced her whole life?

The effect of horrible events is not permanent. Things really happened that way and although we cannot erase any of it, recovery is possible. In Part II we will discover that the traumas are not where the stories end.

Part II

**Discussions with People
Who Have Survived
Extreme Abuse
and
Their Therapy Partners**

CHAPTER 7:

Anna— The Truth Will Set You Free

Hurdles are made for leaping, bridges are made for crossing, and pathways are made for following. But sometimes, hurdles appear where least expected, canyons are encountered with no bridges spanning them, and the wilderness fans out ahead without a pathway. No one has been there before. The terrain is unknown and although danger seems near, the traveler must press ahead. It is destiny. The quality of life must be better beyond the wilderness.

When I met Anna, she had already passed some hurdles and canyons with the assistance of a therapist, and called on me to guide her through the remaining uncharted territory. She told me how the former therapist helped discover her dissociative process and helped build cooperation into her personality system. But, three years ago, that therapist was not yet ready to take her into the territory ahead, so Anna asked if I would be interested. I invited her to bring her husband along so we could assess things together.

Her husband (Gerald), Anna, and I have been working our way through unknown territory since that time. The work is sometimes frightening and the journey has been long, but obstacles have not deterred Anna from forging ahead. She is very consistent in therapy, and continues to keep other commitments in her rich life. She is working on a masters degree in counseling, is in the middle of an internship, and enjoys relationships with Gerald, their children, and grandchildren.

Life with the Wrong Diagnosis

JIM: What was life like before you found out you were dissociative?

ANNA: I tried to maintain my responsibilities in life. Because I was married at sixteen and had a baby at seventeen, I had to grow up fast. I read a lot of self-help books. The problems I was having then were severe depression, suicidal thoughts, fear and anxieties, and even rage. So, on one hand, I was on top of things as far as maintaining my role as a wife and as a mother. On the other hand, when I was alone I would fall apart.

I saw a psychiatrist starting at age nineteen for about nine years, and was medicated for most of that time with anti-depressants. What finally stopped therapy was a spiritual experience. I began to put a lot of focus on spirituality, using that area to develop new coping skills. Managing anger was a priority, as well as spending quiet time in meditation and prayer.

Eventually, I was able to put away most of my fears and anxieties. For a period of about three years things calmed down. I did not feel overwhelmed and had no significant distress, but the old feelings of being out of control did return.

I started seeing a Christian counselor and during that time my dissociativeness became more prominent. I was leading women's Bible studies, co-leading a Sunday school class with my husband, and providing lay counseling at my church. But, I was more depressed and more suicidal than ever. I was "losing it" when I was alone. After running from wall to wall, crying out in terror, I would collapse on the floor, sobbing, not knowing what was wrong with me. It went on like that for about three and a half years.

JIM: Did your husband know this was happening?

ANNA: Yes. He was the only one who knew. My two children—a teen and a preteen at that time—had no idea that I was suicidal or depressed, because my dissociativeness was working so well. I could be on the floor sobbing five minutes before they would get home from school, and before they got home, I would make it to the kitchen, I'd give them a snack and talk to them about their day. They thought everything was fine.

After that, I had an intense spiritual and psychological crisis, and had to take a sabbatical for several months. I pretty much shut down, dissociated emotionally from everything and everyone. Eventually, I began to function again, went back to work, and got back into leading small groups, but I was very separate at the feeling level in all areas of my life.

Flashbacks Signal the Correct Diagnosis

ANNA: About four years ago, I began to have the old symptoms—depression, fears, and anxieties were constant. I went into a hospital to work on some emerging memories which were beyond anything I had ever heard of. They were flashbacks. I was switching into some of the parts that had been put away for years. After I would be in those parts, I would forget what had happened. It was my husband who pointed this out to me, which prompted me to seek help. I knew it was beyond what I could do on my own.

JIM: Did they pick up the dissociation when you were hospitalized?

ANNA: Yes. In the hospital I was assigned to a woman counselor, a psychologist, a psychiatrist, and some other group leaders who were part of my treatment team. The woman counselor diagnosed me by the second week, and for five weeks we did intense memory work. Many of my parts began to relive the experiences. We brought them a lot of healing.

JIM: What happened in therapy after you got out of the hospital?

ANNA: It was very intense. I would be pretty much wiped out after every session. I was acting out a lot— sometimes I would run away, and would literally have to be chased down the street by the therapist and my husband. He went with me to all the sessions, and that was great. It was for him a "hands on" experience, so he would know what to do. The therapy sessions were almost always traumatizing—so intense. It would take a day to recuperate from a session. When I was home I would switch a lot, and parts of me would come out in terror. One very young part crawled over to the door, but couldn't get out because I always kept the doors locked. Other times, I would curl up and be frozen in terror. And I, the host, would not know what it was about. I was "co-present"—I could see what was happening—but I did not have any sense of control. I was in overwhelming fear all the time. I thought I was going crazy. I could not explain it. Without my counselor to remind me that this is normal for what I had been through, and that I was not crazy, I really don't know what I would have done.

During the last five months with the counselor, there were parts of me that were very functional, and although they were not out a whole lot, they were wanting to come out. They were saying, "This is enough. We've got to have a life." I began to have some differences of opinion with the counselor around those issues. Some parts of me wanted to get out and get back into life. It appeared to some parts she wanted to be in control of my therapy to the point where it overlapped into control of my life.

She was extremely busy and unable to keep up with the new information coming into the field of multiple personality disorder. My husband and I were both learning—reading and going to seminars. I was almost becoming my own therapist and her coach!

A New Approach to Multiple Personality

ANNA: In my study, I began to get a new perspective on this condition. Those parts of me that really wanted to be more involved in life were just latching on to whatever we could learn.

JIM: How would you describe that "new perspective"?

ANNA: I learned it was not the end of the world to be dissociative. It was not a negative factor in my life. It was a positive way of coping, and I began to almost have fun with it. I don't want to make it sound frivolous, but I began to experience joy for the first time in a long time. I found the defense mechanism very workable. I was beginning to venture out and accomplish some things in full awareness of my dissociativeness.

JIM: What are the key things to your success since then?

ANNA: First and foremost, to use dissociativeness in a positive way—in a way that will lead to wholeness and a deeper level of congruency in all aspects of my life. I had been given permission to be functional while working through my memories. As I find all my missing parts, I can have a life and live it. I can be back in school, work with people and know it's okay, and then go to therapy to work on the problematic issues.

JIM: You were saving the hard material for therapy and living the rest of your life in your healthy parts?

ANNA: Yes, and I have to say it was hard at first because it ran against everything I had been hearing prior to that. Most of it had been negative. "Now put your life on hold until you're done with therapy!" I rebelled against that. I had so many healthy parts, the new perspective was refreshing for them—it was liberating—and it was strengthening for me to now have a therapist who shared this perspective.

Memory Work

ANNA: Another thing that helped was the way you and I did memory work together. At first it surprised me that I could go into a therapy session, do some hard work, and afterwards the work was continuing in me, but I would switch into my healthy parts and be fine. By the time I got back home I'd be able to have a nice evening, and didn't have to recuperate.

The memory work was done in a way that let me use my dissociativeness to our benefit—not reliving the memory, which had formerly been retraumatizing. That was a significant difference. With the other therapist we were seeking healing. The healing would be there, but there was so much trauma, it would take longer for the healing.

JIM: Can you please give an example?

ANNA: In one particular situation, a part of me had an experience of being filmed during an episode of sexual abuse. She had a difficult time telling about it, so she saw a thick, glass wall separating her from the scene of the memory. Being on this side of the memory, she could see what happened, remember what happened, and talk about it without being in it. She was able to remain separate from it, and didn't have to go into the feelings again. There was some sadness and there was some pain, but the level was minute, compared to being in the middle of it and talking about it while it was happening—a major difference.

She was able to do this well because she had somebody with her—not only her husband, but somebody in the internal world. She had parts and she had spiritual help. She had God with her, and she had inner parts. She could talk about this internally and have people with her; and externally, you, Jim, and her husband were there.

JIM: I think of words like "validation" and "support" and "understanding" and "partners"! All kinds of positive things were going on for her, as opposed to simply reliving the memory.

ANNA: While not reliving it, there was still that sense of reality. It was reality.

JIM: What do you think happened to the feelings in that memory?

ANNA: I believe the feelings were there, because they had been there originally, but they lost their power in the reality of today. Today is also reality. She could tune into the here and now, which lessens the power of the past. It is powerful to be in touch with the here and now, even though I needed to get through the memories for healing and wholeness.

JIM: The fact that it was unknown is important. I believe those who are new to this area have no idea what it is like to find a new memory. What has it been like for you?

ANNA: It was almost like a break from reality. In dissociating, we want to get away from reality. It is so horrendous, so unrealistic, even to imagine horrible things like that could happen when I had no memory of it before—no conscious thoughts. Then to know that it did happen, and know it explained so many other problems, and know that rituals actually did happen! It was hard to look at the depth of the evil that was done to me.

JIM: You said it explained some of your problems. How did some of those things change when the memories were healed?

ANNA: It stopped the behaviors—like I had this

intense need to feel burning. I would want to burn my skin. Mostly it was in the shower. I would find myself turning the water hotter and hotter and hotter until I didn't feel anything. That is not normal behavior! As an adult I knew that was not normal and yet I had no explanation for it. Later we found a particular memory explained why I felt I had to burn myself.

JIM: When you get in the shower now, there is no driving need to get hot anymore?

ANNA: That's right.

JIM: Your heating bill has gone down?

ANNA: Yeah. I told my husband he could turn the water heater lower!

JIM: That may seem a small thing to some people, but that is quite an accomplishment.

ANNA: It really was, because I felt ashamed about it. I was doing something and I didn't know why.

JIM: So how long has it been since you've had a scalding shower?

ANNA: Many months. Those kinds of day-to-day issues I had to deal with no longer take up my time and my energy. It's resolved. It's healed. I'm free from having to hurt myself.

And another thing—I'm free to be in the kitchen now. I don't have to worry about hurting myself with knives. I had a hard time with knives for a long time— an intense fear because I would feel I had to turn that knife on myself. I was afraid I would hurt myself. When we got to the ritual memories, I found in some of the rituals I had to use a knife.

And I'm no longer afraid to be around new people, watching out what they may do. I can just sit there and be part of the group, meet new people, and be comfortable in talking with them. I was always afraid before, always reading people. I was always looking for another motive, like they were going to trick me. I couldn't accept that people would like me just for me.

JIM: What do you think cleared that up?

ANNA: Getting healed from memories where perpetrators tricked me—said they weren't going to hurt me and then they did hurt me. Once those memories surfaced and were healed, I didn't have to be so afraid of people.

JIM: One incident took place in a church, and the perpetrator was a priest. You had felt safe with him, but all of a sudden he turned on you. Would that cause you to be cautious and nontrusting?

ANNA: Yes, especially of men in authority. I belonged to that church and knew this priest. I thought he was representing God to me. Then, during the rituals, he ended up being a perpetrator. If I couldn't trust him, whom could I trust? It took a lot of energy from me to keep trying to read peoples' hidden motives.

Now I'm free, and can participate in whatever is going on. It has been progressive. There were so many times authority figures abused me, and each time one memory was healed, it added to my freedom.

The Spiritual Battle

JIM: Can you please explain the spiritual aspects of your recovery?

ANNA: Because I am in tune with the spiritual dimension of my life, I believe another element was added to the sessions, which brought healing at a deeper level. I think it was important to receive support by being with others who are spiritually inclined. Because I am a spiritual being, I need to be connected at that level as well—not only with God but with people.

JIM: Were there any spiritual obstacles?

ANNA: The horrendous acts that were done, the way the evil just descended to such depths that were beyond any imagination! To know they happened and they were so horrible. For example, having a perpetrator dress up and be portrayed as Jesus. I was raised in a Catholic church and knew about Jesus—the one I was supposed to go to for help. They made it seem he was the one who was hurting me, raping me, doing horrible things to me in this dark, candle-lit place that would escalate to such a frenzy! It was beyond anything my mind could handle. Someone would say, "This is Jesus. This is what God wants for you."

There were so many contradictions given in a direct, overt way. The double messages were causing more dissociating. I would be very, very good and then very, very bad. On one hand, "This is what God wants for you. Be good. Do what God tells you." Then, they would abuse me and say, "You are evil. You are bad."

I lived that way—split into good and bad parts. When I saw the Christian counselor, he would ask about my sense of self and I would always have two answers. I would ask, "Which answer do you want? I have a good answer and I have a bad answer."

He would ask, "Are you going to heaven?"

"Yes I am," I would say. "I am saved by grace. But you know, on the other hand, I'm going straight to hell."

JIM: You were talking honestly from different parts.

ANNA: Absolutely. That was a major inroad perpetrated on my psyche.

JIM: You hit something vital. The purpose of the training—mind control—was to cut you off from grace. You cannot enjoy God's grace if part of you is saying, "I'm on my way to hell." They were taking your joy away from you intentionally.

ANNA: There was never a sense of wholeness in my spirituality. There was always an undermining "dark" aspect which was just as real as the "light" aspect. They wanted me to believe that the dark side is just as powerful as the light side, and the darkness at any point could overwhelm and have the victory. They told me that so many times I believed I would never be able to have perfect peace, or as you put it, enjoy the grace.

JIM: How is the battle going these days?

ANNA: The internal congruency is so much more profound. You know, I don't have to work at it. I don't have to say, "Okay everybody, let's have a meeting here, and decide this." Now it is simply known. Because of the healing, the spirituality is accessible to all of me. We are becoming more and more "one." What is presented to me comes to all of us at one time, and we don't have to have a general meeting. I come to a decision in a more fluid way. We are all like-minded.

The Husband's Contribution to Recovery

JIM: What about your relationship with your husband?

ANNA: I don't feel like I have to manipulate him anymore. I don't find myself having to switch. I can just work on our conflicts as "one." This is really the hardest thing I'm learning right now—what it means to be "one" when I'm stressed in a very personal relationship. But I'm more fluid. I flow. I can be childlike with my husband in one sense, and just flow into whatever is appropriate next, not having to switch. I'm more blended. I see myself like paints, dropping different colors into a bucket, and swirling it. I haven't lost any of my sense of uniqueness in my different aspects. They are all together, and we're always moving. There are always new designs, and that means there are more discoveries. I'm coping with today—not just with negative stresses, but also with challenges, the things that are fun, without having to switch. It flows.

JIM: What happened when some of your parts

who had not met your husband learned to know him? What did they think of him?

ANNA: It would depend. Initially they were very afraid of him. But, my husband is committed to me, and deeply loves me. My parts, young and older, would "check him out." A lot of testing went on. As he would pass each test, they would warm up to him. Some of my parts more recently really didn't want intimacy with him at any level of relationship. However, there was a deep sense of mutual respect between him and my parts, and it had to start with him respecting them. He had to earn their respect. With the younger parts, he had to protect them. That's how he won them over— by showing them he had gone around the house and had put special locks on the doors and windows, and getting an alarm system. We even got a big dog. With the older parts, buying them gifts on the holidays, acknowledging them, validating their presence, and welcoming them into our home.

One time, he took us to a carnival in an area where you were speaking, and we made it a weekend vacation. He said, "Let's go to the carnival." Me, myself, I didn't want to go to the carnival. I wasn't into that, but the little ones loved it. He bought them little things at the carnival. And when little ones would come out and be scared, he would immediately meet their need, reassuring them, talking to them and validating their feelings. Then, he would help them get over the fear and get into the "here and now," so they could see we are safe.

The Effect of the False Memory Controversy

JIM: I keep thinking about the false memory syndrome, and the issue of safety. False memory articles and TV programs can cause safety problems with abuse survivors. How has the false memory controversy affected you?

ANNA: I think the first time I heard about it was on a talk show. Because a representative of a false memory group was a professional, my first reaction was almost a state of panic. I was trying to believe the traumas had happened to me. That was a constant struggle, and now an authority says it's not true! So I'm back to getting two messages, getting two tracks going again! Panic set in.

Something inside would say, "What is happening in my life now and in my therapy, is not reality." I had a terrible struggle to avoid being thrown into denial.

For about five days, I was totally out of touch with the reality of my being dissociative, with the reality of having abuse in my past. I was in a different world, a different state of consciousness. There was a part of me which had no connectedness. I had again completely dissociated. For the first time, I knew what it felt like for those who are told none of this is true, none of this is real, and they buy into it. I had no sense right then of being dissociative, of having memories, or of having a past of abuse.

JIM: And that happened after you saw the talk show?

ANNA: I had read several articles by that time, and the media was reporting more—reporting in a way which carried a lot of authority. And part of my own culture is, "authority rules." This was very disturbing to me. When I finally came out of this state, I was quite shaken up. I had to work hard to get grounded and remain in the here and now.

JIM: You had been put on a collision course with everything you had done in therapy.

ANNA: Oh, yes! When they give accounts so full of authority it has so much power. If we're not careful it will infiltrate, and cause division again—the truth versus cover-up.

JIM: How did you get past that obstacle?

ANNA: So many of my parts had already received healing and had done some good work in therapy, that they pulled me back into reality. I also remained in therapy, talking to people I trust, like you and my husband and close friends, who could once again validate me. When we hear the truth being presented, it begins to release a power that will overcome the lies.

JIM: If an authority says something isn't true about your reality, how is that different from when an authority says your reality is true?

ANNA: There is power in the sense of truth. For people who are dissociative, deep within them is an awareness somewhere inside of the truth. When the truth is spoken, I believe it reaches that place inside which caused us to seek therapy in the first place.

JIM: The Bible says, "You will know the truth and it will set you free" (John 8:32). That is what I count on. I can't get you to accept what seems true to me. You will know it, and when you know it, you will feel free.

ANNA: The truth does cut through the barriers. That is what happened for me when I was coming out of this place of denial where the false memory teachings had brought me. It was the truth that brought back my true self.

JIM: Let me press this issue just a bit further. What do you think happened to the part of you that wanted to stay in denial?

ANNA: I think it got a lot of nurturing. It was interesting to me that everyone inside allowed her to be in that place at first, like she needed to experience life in the here and now. By being allowed to have some space and some time, the truth began to come in to her.

JIM: You didn't hit her over the head with the truth?
ANNA: Oh, no.
JIM: You won her back lovingly?

ANNA: That's right. We let the truth do the work.

JIM: I think some people who would like to contradict us would say, "It's a struggle to know what the truth is. We can never be certain." Do you find it's a struggle to know what the truth is?

ANNA: I think it's a struggle to let go of the lie. It is also a struggle to get to the truth because there are so many lies and so much denial holding people back from the truth. But, when you get to the truth there's freedom. The struggling stops. All of a sudden, you know it's right.

JIM: Anything else you want to say about the false memory controversy?

ANNA: I want to say, "Wake up! Stop hurting people. Don't do this." Any time something is quoted from the false memory groups, it brings confusion and undermines my own work of healing and health. It is invalidating to me as a person, my life, and my experiences. By saying something didn't happen when I know it did, that's crazy-making.

Beyond the Wilderness

JIM: Well, tell me about your future. What do you think about the rest of your life?

ANNA: The most exciting thing is that I don't know, but I know it's good. I'm doing my internship, and I should be graduating with my masters degree in a few months. I see myself doing more and enjoying more. I don't mean just doing more work. I want to have more fun too, in everything I do! And I love speaking. I have had a taste of it and I will probably continue doing that. I love to teach.

I'm going to be knocking on a lot of doors, and it's exciting to know I can do that. I don't have anything to hide. For so many years, I had to keep things hidden. Now I am flinging the doors open, the windows open, and I can invite people into my life without fear. I know there is evil out there. I will probably always be exposed to that, but I don't have to let it be a part of my life anymore. I can go out and test relationships and know I have all I need to be successful and to be fulfilled. Because I've been able to do a lot of neat things in my past, I have had a sense of fulfillment. The difference is, I can do this now with more wholeness, without being pulled in a different direction. I am more focused.

JIM: During the last three years, you have been doing things successfully all along. It is not like therapy gave you success, therapy just helped you refine it. You were already doing things you were good at—leading groups, speaking, being a career person, a wife and a mother. You never stopped doing those things.

ANNA: I needed to be given permission, and at some point I had to give myself permission to take control of my life. I needed to overcome whatever was blocking me from doing all those things to the best of my ability. Life is for living, and I want to live it in truth and just enjoy the freedom which comes from that.

CHAPTER 8:

Where Were You, God?

Gloria— Making a Difference

The list of people who have asked me why God let them suffer is long, as is the list of those who asked God to stop the abuse while it was happening. It remains a mystery. How can bad things happen if God is good?

The ancient story of Job's suffering explores this question extensively and concludes its best answer comes directly from God. Job was a prosperous and happy man, blessed with a wonderful family. He lost everything, including his family, and was smitten with horrible diseases. After Job and his friends did their best to make sense out of his suffering, they challenged God—He must have made a mistake. God spoke to them, most eloquently, of His majesty. He revealed to Job that He rules the universe with wisdom and power, and equips His creatures to live a meaningful life in the world He created.

Job could only reply, "I know that you can do all things; no plan of yours can be thwarted. . . . Surely I spoke of things I did not understand, things too wonderful for me to know. . . . My ears had heard of you but now my eyes have seen you." Job humbled himself before the Lord, prayed that his friends would also be forgiven, and the Lord richly blessed him once again.[1]

I believe God still gives us answers to questions we struggle with, still equips us to live meaningful lives, and He still blesses those who humbly seek Him. This chapter is about how God blessed Gloria.

JIM: I remember a time in my office, Gloria, when you and I talked about Job's question, "Why does God allow suffering?" I forget exactly how long ago it was—over two years. As I remember, you processed a memory with me and at the conclusion, here is what you said: "God told me that when I went to live with Aunt Agnes (ages two to ten) she and her family could do anything to me she chose, and God would not stop her. But, like any parent who can see their child being abused, without being able to stop it, He was suffering too. He promised that He would heal me." Is that the way you remember it?

GLORIA: (Gloria had a good laugh while her husband, William, and I awaited her answer.) You missed the whole thing! Actually, you got the gist of it, but you forgot where it happened. It happened in my prayer group at home. I just told you about it in your office. (What an interesting development! My memory of the event was incorrect. If I had testified about this in court, my account would have been thrown out—I missed some peripheral details, like where it happened).

I had asked God earlier why these things had happened. He kept telling me He loved me, and that He was with me while it all happened. At that time I only knew about sexual abuse in my life, (she later discovered she had also been through ritual abuse) but I was infuriated at His answer! "What do you mean, you were there? Fat lot of good it did me!"

He said, "Well, here, I'll show you." I could see this—it was like a vision. God said, "Imagine you are in a room with your daughter when she is about three, and there is a group of men with her. You are tied to a column with both hands tied behind your back. You cannot do anything to help her, but you can see the men with your daughter and hear your daughter's cries. She can't see that you're tied and continues crying for your help."

Then He asked me how I felt. I just started crying. I was devastated. The pain caused by my daughter not understanding why I was not coming to her aid, was as great or greater than the pain of watching the men hurt her, because she thought I did not love her.

Then the scene switched. I was the one being hurt, He was tied up at the post, and He was crying. He said, "I was there. I saw it all. I felt it all. It hurt me, but I would not manipulate their free will to choose. I gave your mother and father spiritual authority over you, and they chose to give you to aunt Agnes and her family. Your parents transferred authority to wicked people—people who gave their wills over to wickedness. I did not change their wills even though I did work through circumstances on your behalf, and I never left you."

Then He said, "I was just waiting until I could get your will. Your will was captive by their's because you were so young. But, the minute I could get into your heart, I was so happy that I could in earnest begin my plan in your life."

I just melted to the ground. Every ounce of bitterness and anger went out of me. I knew He didn't want this. I knew He didn't cause, plan, or purpose this evil. I knew He was for me, and here He was now, getting ready to answer the prayers I prayed as a child. It may have taken years, but He didn't forget.

Ritual Abuse Emerges

JIM: You said at that time you knew only about sexual abuse. How did it first come to you that there was something beyond sexual abuse?

GLORIA: My first memory of ritual abuse started with a body memory.[2] I couldn't sleep one night. I had so much pain across my neck and shoulders—terrible pain. I was in prayer. "God, I can't stand this pain. What is it?" All of a sudden, I was having this flashback. I was hanging on a cross, tied to it, and my head was hanging. My arms were up, and that's why my neck was so tired. I was about three, and I was saying in this tiny little voice, "Couldn't I please get down? Please could you let me down?" A woman with a black robe on was coming at me with a chalice full of blood.

I asked myself, "How could these things be? What is this? Did I make this up? Is something playing with my mind?" I was terrified, but at the same time, I wasn't terrified because the Lord was there. I couldn't find any cubby-hole in which to shove this thing. It was ugly. I didn't know what to do with it.

JIM: Had you been in therapy by then?

GLORIA: No, and I didn't know anything about ritual abuse. I think I knew vaguely that there were people who worshipped Satan. But I thought they met in a church, made fun of the Lord's supper, sang hymns backwards or something, and had seances. I didn't really know what they did. I'd never heard of such a thing as SRA.

JIM: What happened after you got this memory that didn't fit anywhere?

GLORIA: The problems already in my life escalated. I was awakened with night terrors. I would be lying on my back with the covers up to my chin, and all of a sudden, I would feel the weight of the covers as though it was ten tons of dirt, and I would wake up terrified of being buried alive. I would sit bolt upright. I couldn't stay under those covers. I would pray, "The Lord is my shepherd." I did not know what the terror was. It was following me hard and it was all over me. Eventually, fear and terror consumed me to the point that they invaded every detail of my daily life and I was unable to function.

JIM: How long ago was that?

WILLIAM: About four years ago.

JIM: How did you make sense out of her suffering, William?

WILLIAM: I didn't. I was hurt and confused because there were so many aspects of Gloria. I didn't know enough to see how abnormal this was. I think I was as supportive as I could be.

GLORIA: Yes, he was. We were always for each other. We were always best friends. We just didn't know what to do. We had so few resources.

Dominoes

JIM: What are some things you did to find help?

GLORIA: Over the course of twenty years—from ages ten to thirty—I looked desperately for answers. I probably tried every religion and every pop psychology movement. There was this deep need in me and a growing pain that nothing was touching. And I tried two therapists.

JIM: What happened there?

GLORIA: After an initial assessment, one therapist wrote to me, refusing to treat me, saying I was psychotic, and he couldn't help me. The other psychiatrist tried to seduce me, and I left him.

By the time I met you, it was eighteen years after my brief encounter with the other therapists. When I met you, I was having so many flashbacks and recurring dreams and fragmented memories—like having one corner of a puzzle and a piece or two out of the middle, but nothing else! I was in an anatomy and physiology class, and I had to work with a cadaver. That was God's hammer that just shattered the amnesia. It was like having an internal earthquake. Walls cracked and crumbled.

I started having overwhelming emotions, and pictures—flashes of pieces of things: a skull, a goat's foot, an open grave, bodies, dark things, and lots of strange thoughts about Satan. But mostly, it was emotional. I could not hold myself together. I thought I was a strong person, because I could hold myself together through anything up to that point. That was my specialty. Get through this, then face that, and face the next thing. That's how I lived. I never saw beyond the present. I never saw a future. I lived moment to moment, crisis to crisis, but I couldn't deal with the cadaver. It was time for God to heal me.

In the meantime, I was meeting with two ladies from church each week. This was months before I met you. We would pray and talk about intimate things together. While we were praying over me we got this word, "dissociation." We didn't know what it meant. We didn't even look it up in the dictionary for some reason.

Then, another morning I woke up, and just clear as a bell I heard the Holy Spirit say to me, "distinct personalities."

JIM: You knew what that meant?

GLORIA: Not really. I'd always wondered if there were two of me. Maybe I was a split person, divided down the middle. One part was good and one was bad, and if the bad part ever got out, it was going to swallow the rest of me. That was in the back of my mind, an unspoken, buried fear.

JIM: Did she tell you about this, William?

WILLIAM: No, but Gloria and I did have an awareness of an older self and a younger self—a little Gloria. We started honoring the little Gloria. I would bring her presents—things appropriate for a child. We didn't think of it as anything other than "Little Gloria."

GLORIA: It wasn't as though I had a different personality. It was a left-over piece of childhood or something. One day, I was sewing, making a straight seam and it went all crooked. I said, "Now, Gloria, can't you do anything right?" The minute I said that, I felt fear jump up in me, and I started speaking against fear, as if it had come from outside of me. And the Spirit of the Lord said, "That's not the spirit of fear. That's Little Gloria! She was trying to sew and you yelled at her and made her afraid."

I said, "Well, what am I supposed to do then?"

He said, "Just go stand in front of a mirror and apologize to her. Tell her you're sorry. You shouldn't have yelled at her like that."

So I did. "I'm sorry, little girl, I didn't know you were there! I didn't mean to hurt you." She calmed right down.

From that point on, He started helping this little Gloria part. She would come out when I was on a walk or something. I started telling my friends about little Gloria. I had this "child within" concept.

JIM: How did you decide to start therapy with me?

GLORIA: Things had gotten so bad between not sleeping anymore, having terror and horror in the night, and not being able to concentrate at school or work. A psychologist was speaking at a college not far away and my pastor asked him to come speak to us. He talked about satanic ritual abuse and multiple personality. I'd never heard of either one. I'd heard of multiple personality, but only from the movies, *Three Faces of Eve* and *Sybil*.

The more he talked, the more it felt like he was hammering nails in my coffin. He described indicators in a person's life who had been ritualized. I had every one of them. When he said those things, they registered. Like someone was fitting round pegs in round holes! Click, click, click! When something registers like that, you know that you know that you know.

WILLIAM: The thing he came to talk about was the

reality of ritual abuse, and not so much about multiple personality. The gist of his talk was, "This stuff is real." His wife was a survivor.

GLORIA: God had it all lined up, Jim. It was just like dominoes. On my way to the healing conference where I heard you speak, this came out of my mouth: "If they had a workshop on multiple personality, I would take it." I didn't know what I was saying! I was desperate: violent headaches, I couldn't focus my eyes, couldn't sleep, was full of memories, flashbacks, terrors in the night. I was falling apart! I went there looking for a miracle.

The first thing I saw at the conference was a sign which said "Multiple Personality Workshop." God was at work to provide for my healing and to answer my childhood prayers. So I went to the class. During a break, I went up to you and asked, "Could I have one of your business cards?" You said, "Sure," but I didn't trust you. Something inside said, "He doesn't like me. I don't think he really wants me to have one." When I got home, I couldn't find the card!

JIM: Someone inside trashed it.

GLORIA: Someone trashed that card good, but I was terrified, because now I couldn't reach you. I called to the conference every day that week, and nobody knew how to get you. I was desperate because I knew from taking your workshop that I needed your help. I was a thread away from insanity. While I was picking up the phone on Friday, the last day of the confer- ence, I said, "Lord, you're going to have to do it now. It's now or never." The man on the phone said he would not be able to find Dr. Friesen, and could I call back after the conference? I told him, "No, I need him now." I felt, literally, I could not make it to Monday. Just then, I had a vision in which I saw you walk up to his desk. Through the vision, God gave me a mea- sure of peace. About thirty minutes later, he called me back and said, "You'll never guess what happened! Dr. Friesen walked up to my desk and asked if he could use the phone." Then he gave me your phone number.

JIM: That's the way God works. He brings the right people together at the right time, and we all know who sets up the dominoes!

GLORIA: We got your book and read it at once. We'd been married for twenty-some years, wondering at all these puzzle pieces, trying to figure out why one minute I'd say something and then say I didn't say it. William was so relieved. He said, "Gloria, this is what we've been waiting for all our lives!" The book was like cold water to a dry and thirsty desert traveler.

Are My Memories True?

JIM: When memories started coming to you, did they seem they could be true? You said you had no place to put them.

GLORIA: I had all sorts of thoughts and feelings. I had a divided mind about it. Fancy that! I believed it must be true because of the presence of the Lord, but my rational mind found it terribly hard to accept. As I would go over the memories of my childhood, I would ask myself, "Where does this fit?" Where could this possibly have happened? I just could not put the ritual memories in anywhere. It seemed so unreal, it seemed like a vicious trick somebody was playing on me, or my own mind was playing on me. I thought, "I'm way off the scale! I've invented a new thing!"

But, I knew I could trust the Lord, and as I asked Him about these things I felt His assurance over and over, not to run, not to be afraid, to just trust Him and to keep walking. Since then I've remembered where and how most of the things fit in.

JIM: Could you describe the process of how the memories first seemed untrue and then, after a while, they began to feel true?

GLORIA: It was a difficult process. The more I experienced healing for the memories, the more I knew they were true, because of the fruit that came from the healing. I changed. I could look people in the eye and not look down. Shame had left me. That seems like a small thing, but it was big. I could now have conversations without my mind checking out altogether. There were many things about my personality that changed directly as a result of the healing.

JIM: You mean, from practically each memory that received healing, there were some things in your daily life. . . .

GLORIA: Not "practically" from each memory, from each healed memory, I had direct fruit. One was being able to sleep. After I saw you for two or three visits, I began to be able to sleep through the night. I hadn't done that in years. I would sleep ten minutes and wake up terrified. Then I'd be up for two or three hours, sleep fifteen minutes, and wake up terrified. I never slept more than about twenty minutes.

WILLIAM: Through the process of therapy, I started to meet personalities I had known all along. I was meeting as separate personalities these different aspects of Gloria which were very familiar to me. That told me we're dealing with real stuff—the voice changes, face changes, how they each would sit.

JIM: You have been very dedicated to Gloria's therapy. You haven't missed very many therapy sessions in three years.

WILLIAM: Not a one.

JIM: What has been drawing you so strongly to participate?

WILLIAM: This is finally the unfolding of our lives. It is helping Gloria become the person she has always deserved to be.

It's my healing too. I'm learning things about myself, drawing closer to God, and going through healing of my own. Another thing God orchestrated was that I became a believer six months before this process started. In a sense, it all had to wait on that. This has been a "fast track" course for me in gaining a really deep belief in God. He has worked miracles.

GLORIA: I can't even describe how important William has been. He's always believed in me and he's always tried to bring the best out in me. This is just more of that. He's just loving me. He's really important to all my people—every one of them knows him. The little ones love and appreciate him so much, and look up to him.

About "False Memories"

JIM: Have people tried to help you by suggesting your issues may be nothing more than "false memories"?

GLORIA: My memories have been discounted frequently.

JIM: What impact did that have?

GLORIA: The first thing was anger, then right behind it, fear. It was unsettling. I think it revictimized me, because horrible things have happened to me, and now someone has the audacity to not believe me, and minimize my feelings. It put me in jeopardy and made me doubt myself.

I don't know how to make someone believe this. I can only say what happened to me, and I can only say what therapy has done for me. I am freer. Life was as though I had tons of baggage hanging on me. I would try to walk, but could not get very far. One tiny step required such effort! Therapy has lifted those things off. I'm so much lighter. Life is now a joy.

JIM: How does the false memory controversy affect you, William?

WILLIAM: It angers me to see what they're doing,

helping people who are in denial to stay there, and trying to upset legitimate therapy.

GLORIA: I don't have any interest whatsoever in suing anybody. I wouldn't even waste my time. That would rob me of time I can be creating beautiful things. All I want is to be free. I want to be me. I want to live my life, and exercise the talents and abilities God has given me, freely. So, I'm in this process with many helpers—my husband, my therapist, my children, my friends, my pastor, and we are stripping away the things that keep me from doing that.

Community

JIM: You mentioned the involvement of your pastor and your church—your community. You go to a church that's more open to this area than most churches. They are very supportive. How important is that to you?

GLORIA: It would have absolutely killed me if they had not been able to accept my diagnosis. It would have crushed me. Maybe I would have had power and strength from God to get up and go through the therapy anyway, but I would have had to cut myself off completely from a body of people I love. I couldn't have continued to be with them if they didn't believe it, because it's my life. Having relationships with people, you share your life together. If they had not been able to say they understand and support me, it would have ground me into powder. It's been very important to me! I've had a whole community of people supporting me, understanding me when I get triggered sometimes, people I can call if I get into a hard spot, people who have learned to help my little ones when they show up.

JIM: You remember what you said about dominoes? You are in a church which can accept this, your husband became a believer, you were required to take an anatomy course, you went to the right conference, and you got the right person on the phone. There was always a domino in the right place.

GLORIA: Every time. That's because God is who He says He is. He's faithful and He's loving and He has our healing in His heart. He's interested in us. He wants to heal us. He wants to give us life. He wants us to be full of His joy. Joy is one of the fruits I receive after each healing. You ask how I know this is real? I used to be one of the most depressed persons. I would get into one of those spirals, and be down there for weeks. I couldn't even get out of bed. And now, I'm like a house afire. I have joy. I'm glad to be alive. This is a miracle! I actually like who I am! I used to hate myself. I loathed myself. I'm beginning to know who I am, and I like what I see. I'm not depressed. I'm not wanting to die every five minutes. I wanted to leave this earth. I didn't see anything to stay for. But I want to stay now. I want to make a difference.

Making a Difference

JIM: Tell me about the ways you are giving back to your community.

GLORIA: I became part of a group for abused women for two and a half years, and I was able to be a co-facilitator in that group as a result of the healing I received. I have a strong desire in my heart to help people, particularly abused people, and more particularly, children. I want to let them know how special they are, how valuable they are, how loved they are by God, and to just put some kind of seed in there for these little kids.

I had seeds sown in me when I was little. God, somehow, got the seed of His Word in me. The Bible says the Word of God is incorruptible—cannot be destroyed. They already tried to destroy the Word of God. They hung it on the cross and buried it in a tomb, but it came right back. It's incorruptible. The deep beliefs I had about myself as a child, and about the goodness of God, came from somewhere. Somebody told me something. I always tell little children things like, "Do you know how special you are?" or just some little word of encouragement to build them up.

One lady did something for me when I was a child that I've never forgotten. I was being forced to eat my lunch, and I was supposed to eat everything. I had eaten it all except this tall glass of milk. I was stuffed, and I was about to throw up. Aunt Agnes said, "Drink it!" and then she left the room. A visitor came through the room, saw me sitting there in tears, and leaned down. She asked, "What's the matter?" I said, "I've got to drink this milk and I'm too full."

She picked up that glass and drank it down, winked at me and set it back on the table. I've never forgotten that. It was a tiny act of kindness to a child. Nobody had ever done anything like that for me before. When I'm around children, I always want to tell them how important they are. I want to place the incorruptible seed in little children. They're such treasures!

WILLIAM: We've looked around for ways to help others. Gloria has done this group for abused women. We've tried to get a group for survivors and their spouses which didn't last very long. A year ago three of us men got together in a prayer group, and being led by the Lord to add one other man. Three of the four of us are spouses of survivors and we are support for each other. It's important in a lot of ways that we've been brought together.

GLORIA: There's also been a lot of "one-on-one" help. God really sends people to us. That's one of the biggest offshoots of this therapy for me. I can give hope to people who are desperate. I can say, "I used to be there and now I'm here." I really appreciate what therapy has given me—I can give hope to others.

WILLIAM: I think it's really important what we're doing today to expose the lies spread by false memory groups, because to the extent that it would shut down any therapist—scare them off or bankrupt them—that hope is cut off for some people. A lot of things happened to free Gloria. God orchestrated it all, but part of that plan was you being here, Jim. If you were not willing to pursue this work, that would have been an obstacle for Gloria and me in realizing this miracle.

GLORIA: If you had been shut down in the middle of my therapy, I'd hate to think what would have happened to me. I'd be wandering the streets, or in the state hospital, terrified and hopeless.

WILLIAM: Or dead.

JIM: If therapists fear they may be sued, or if they are convinced to disbelieve what they see, they will not do the things they need to do, and their clients will not receive the hope they deserve to receive. I guess I have to look at this through the eyes of a believer—God brings certain people to me; I know it is His doing, and I've got to work with them, even if I have reservations. If therapists have clients who ask, "Can you get me down from this cross, please?" and they say, "I'm sorry, I don't do that," I think they are not being the person they were meant to be, and are missing the blessing of fulfilling their destiny.

GLORIA: And it is a blessing. When I have been able to help survivors get through memories or to give them other support, it has been a thrill to see them becoming free, joyful, productive people. The privilege of participating in that sort of transformation can only be called a blessing.

CHAPTER 9:

Depression

Therapy can become intense, progress is usually slow, and physical problems are often a handicap. Discouragement and depression are almost inevitable.

Millie and Laura— Partners for Life

When a client develops depression, I find it useful to follow principles taught by psychologists Thomas Brownback and Linda Mason:[1] People operate in a depressed mode if basic needs in four areas go unmet, so they train clients to meet those needs every day.

—Biological (nutrition, sleep, exercise, and relaxation)

—Psychological (journaling, reading for growth, self-affirmation, and attention to addictions)

—Social (conflict resolution, sharing, fun, and affirming others)

—Spiritual (worship, Bible time, prayer, and Christian music)

Through the years, I have come to recognize how important spiritual and social needs are for abuse survivors, particularly when depressed. At the clinic where I work, we have found clients do better if supportive friends are present in therapy, especially if they share a spiritual commitment. A few years ago, it seemed unrealistic to have clients invite someone to join them during their sessions, but over time, our conviction grew that it is a benefit to bring a trusted friend to every session. During the last four years, I have let my clients know they will do best if they hook up with a therapy partner who can attend each session and be available for regular contact outside of therapy.

I continue to see good results, particularly in the areas of social and spiritual needs. Clients still may get depressed and steady progress is not guaranteed, but life is less burdensome when shared with a therapy partner.

Millie

Getting Started as a Partner

JIM: It has been over four years since you started out as a partner. You are a veteran! I have found your eagerness refreshing, but your wondrous mind comes up with too many questions. Actually, I believe you bring up questions I need to think about, so to be honest, your questions are extremely helpful. How did you become a therapy partner in the first place?

MILLIE: I met Laura quite by God's design. There is no particular reason we should have connected, but we met in one common area of our interest; working out at the gym.

Our first conversation was a total disaster, and I don't think either of us expected our relationship to go anywhere, but it did. As we began to develop our relationship, we talked about some of the current struggles Laura was having. At that time, the only thing we were aware of was the eating disorder. She had been hospitalized and treated, and was looking for someone to help her with anorexia. I felt totally inadequate when she asked if I would be the person to whom she could be accountable. I had reservations. I tend to be a person who doesn't commit to things lightly, and it's important for me to follow through.

So I prayed about it, talked to my husband, and got what I call "green lights." So, I went back to her and said, "Well, I don't know what to do to help you, but I'm willing."

She said, "Don't worry about it. Just be there when I call. If I call you, that's going to help me get through. Just talk to me."

I said, "Okay, I can do that."

That gave her freedom to call, and she did. We continued to enjoy each other. We could tell something was happening in our relationship, but we didn't know what. We didn't rush it, and as God would have it, things got worse! They absolutely got worse. She became extremely depressed and suicidal. At that point, I started to wonder whether I was more help or trouble. I talked to a couple of counselors. They encouraged me to stay involved, and not to take on her problem as my problem. I sort of understood that, but you can't help but hurt when somebody's hurting.

Her situation deteriorated so much that she decided she wanted get into one-on-one counseling. She would get back from a session with you and I would ask, "So, how did it go?", and she'd tell me as much as she understood about it. She was supposed to talk about the different roles she had in life, and there was something about a little girl, something about parts, and I listened and tried to understand. Finally, she just said, "Why don't you come with me?"

I said, "Come with you? I've never heard of such a thing. Why don't you check with your counselor." She said it was your idea, so I began to come along to each session. That was January of 1991. Soon, you gave us each a copy of your book, *Uncovering the Mystery of MPD*, we both read it, and asked, "Now what does this mean?" [This is a bit of tongue-in-cheek humor.]

JIM: When you came to therapy with Laura, did it seem you belonged right there at her side?

MILLIE: Surprisingly, it felt very natural to be in a counseling session together. It was nice because I would hear firsthand, and then we could talk about it and extend it, and come up with ideas and applications and questions together that probably would have taken a lot longer to surface. We spent a lot of time on those issues.

Over the last four years, we have tried to keep counseling day as our day as much as possible. It's nice to just block out that day and do whatever together. Sometimes, we go sit at the park and talk, sometimes, we go shopping, just being together and letting what needs to happen, happen.

JIM: You have a good time together, don't you?

MILLIE: We have a really good time together. I was forty-seven years old then, and was introduced to the word "play." My husband and I could have fun, but Laura and I would have a "play day." Many of the people around us have picked up that term—play day. Parts of Laura would call it "Millie day."

A Friend Who Dissociates

JIM: So you'd play all day after an early morning therapy session. Therapy wasn't very much different from the rest of your life. She was dissociating between some of her parts in therapy, and outside of therapy, too. It was okay for her to be in any part she needed to be.

MILLIE: Absolutely; and I like the way you put it, "needed to be." She needs to be in certain parts in order to communicate what's going on inside, that can't be communicated by other parts.

JIM: Did you find it difficult to get a handle on how to relate to a person who dissociates?

MILLIE: I don't think I had any trouble at all. I enjoy the angry teen-agers the most. I could really identify with those angry teenagers. I probably had the hardest time with the children. Pain is more an adult issue. Getting back into the pain of being a child, in this case, pain beyond anything I'd ever thought about—that was the hardest.

JIM: During a ten-day period, Christmas of 1991, Laura had a happy child out. That was ten days of jubilation. It was Christmas, and it was heavenly.

MILLIE: It was fun! It was delightful.

JIM: The other child parts who were in such pain were the ones you were having a hard time relating to, but not the happy child?

MILLIE: All child parts are hard for me. I don't relate well to children in general. I like them fine. I was an only child until I was ten years old, raised by a very adult family. When I turned forty my husband said, "You finally became the age you always were!" It's been a challenge for me to relate to the children, but I'm learning.

JIM: Can you describe your relationship with one of the child parts?

MILLIE: There's one that's about seven that is probably one of the most vocal, and able to communicate child needs. These days, she is probably the one I have the most contact with. In the beginning there was a three-year-old, and I still communicate with the three-year-old, but mostly with the seven-year-old. Then there's a smaller one, probably two-ish.

JIM: "Me Ma?"

MILLIE: Me Ma, to whom I have become, "Me Ma" [my mother]. She gets down to the most basic need, to be held, and is most free to ask, "Please hold me."

She needs to look in my eyes a lot. Sometimes she reaches up and hugs me around the neck and says, "I love you, Me Ma. I love you, Me Ma." Part of Laura was stuck at that age, not receiving enough love. Now she is able to experience some of the warmth children need. The little ones will ask, "Are you going away? How much do you love me? Will you hold me? Can I get next to you?" They seem to enjoy very much having some freedom to touch and be touched, things she probably needed to experience as a child.

Ritualized Child Parts

JIM: What's it like to be with the seven-year-old? Give a thumbnail sketch of her.

MILLIE: She's bright and eager to talk. In the beginning, she was afraid of talking. A lot was programmed into her. In her SRA background it was simple—you don't talk. She has overcome a lot of that, but she still has a ways to go. She has a lot of questions about all kinds of things; some I don't know how to answer at the child level. Things have happened to her that should never happen to children. She has questions that children should never have to think about.

JIM: What kind of questions?

MILLIE: Sexual questions, cruelty questions, abandonment questions, things that children should not even know about at that age.

JIM: It is staggering to put oneself in that position. I try to see things through the eyes of a seven-year-old who has been through that, and I cannot do it.

MILLIE: I can only listen and ask God to give me sensitivity. God has used it to deepen my relationship with Him. As she has asked God questions, I have had to ask God questions. "Where were you? Do you really love us?" Those questions are too real to be dismissed. It has affected my relationship with God in the most profound way, of anything that has happened in my life.

Relationships

MILLIE: I knew little about the meaning of relationship before I met Laura. We laughingly call me a closet person, and He used her to unlock my door, draw me out, and it has radically changed my concept of God. It was probably the beginning of a profound thing—getting to know who am I—my identity. After knowing Laura for about six months, some of the sexual abuse issues had come up, not the SRA stuff yet, so we'd gone from eating disorders to sexual issues, and I was going deeper and deeper into this. "Oh, my gosh, what in the world is going on?"

I went to a seminar on recovery from sexual abuse just to find out what are some of the dynamics at play here? It was a Christian seminar led by a person I have come to admire. The doctor who led that seminar laid down what you might call a model for how he sees the human personality—just who are we and what is life about? He talked about who we are as a child of God. I could have told you before that I was a child of God. If you would have asked me if I was a child of God, I would have said, "Of course. It says so in the Bible." I had no concept what that meant. He went on to say we are created in the image of our Father. So I'm going from, "Wow, I'm a child of God!" to "How am I made? What kind of image am I made in, what is this image thing, what are you talking about?"

JIM: You ask the right questions!

MILLIE: Well, that's how my mind goes all the time, believe me. If I asked questions all day long, they would be one millionth of what's going on in my head. So, while I'm still asking these questions, he's saying to be created in His image is to be created for relationship.

"Relationship? Me, the closet person?" As I grew up, I learned to make aloneness my friend. I began to ask, "You mean I'm not living according to my design, like a squirrel trying to be a duck?" I had been trying to live according to my own design. He said God is so relational, He's in relationship with Himself—the Father, the Son, and the Holy Spirit. He wants us being in relationship with Him, Him being in relationship with us, and us being in relationship with each other. I didn't live like that before then at all, but now I knew that is what I was created for. I was almost fifty years old.

Then, I remembered praying when I was twenty-five, a year after I came to know the Lord. I was aware of my immaturity and I remember praying, "Lord, I want to grow up. I don't care what it takes. If I get halfway through and say I don't want to grow anymore, don't pay any attention to me. Do whatever it takes." God brought that prayer to remembrance, and said, "This is it." He had put this person into my life to begin to experience relationship.

JIM: When you two have a "play day," people say, "Oh, they're sisters! They must be sisters—they have so much fun together."

MILLIE: Almost everyone asks if we're related—if we're sisters, if I'm her mother, if we are twins, and there's eleven years difference! Just a couple of days ago, there was a gal at the gym who said, "I'm so used to seeing you two together. Whenever I see one of you, I always look to see where the other one is." People are used to seeing us together. God has really bonded our relationship, and I suspect it has planted a desire in others for this thing called relationship with God and each other.

JIM: Did you feel like sisters for a while? Since you

knew mostly "only child" feelings, would you know what a sister feels like?

MILLIE: I have two sisters who are ten and twelve years younger, so I was more of a mother to them than a sister. Laura and I don't have those growing-up things in common. I don't know a lot about sisters. Laura, on the other hand, had a very difficult sister relationship. We started out as friends, and I'm the one who said for about the first year or so, "That's all I want—to have a friend and be a friend."

I've had so many people say, "I'm glad you're helping Laura," or "I'm so glad you have a ministry with Laura." I appreciated their intent. I didn't take offense with them, but hearing the words, somehow, did not represent what was happening. I wasn't helping her. I was enjoying her, and if help came out of that, great. Believe me, there were times help didn't come out of that. I was aware I wasn't always helping. I don't have enough self-confidence to think I can help anybody, and I wasn't ministering to Laura.

Once I learned who I was as a child of God, and how I was created in His image, I said, "I just want two things out of life. I just want to be loved and enjoyed. Anybody that can do that, wow! I realized I'm hard to love and hard to enjoy at times. To the extent people can give me that, God bless 'em. Sometimes I'll tease Laura if she's going through a tough time, not wanting to talk to me. I'll say something to her along the lines of, "You're missing a blessing!" (Millie's voice intonation is young and cute.)

She'll say, "What do you mean?"

(The cute voice continues.) "You could be enjoying me or loving me, certainly you could find something in me to enjoy!" It kind of coaxes her out of things.

Adoption

MILLIE: Laura has adopted into my biological family, and they have adopted her. She's more the age of my sisters, and they think she's the greatest thing that ever happened to me. Being involved with her has changed my life, and I'm a better big sister to them than I ever was, and they'll tell you that in a minute. "We're so glad Laura's in your life! You were a pain in the neck!"

JIM: How did the adoption come about?

MILLIE: I was sitting in church one night when we'd gone from friend to sister to soul mate. Laura was with me and my biological sister was there. They were laughing and carrying on and having a good time and I looked at them. I had seen Laura struggle through so much pain, but now she was laughing from the bottom of her toes, and giggling and carrying on. I had this sweep, this wave, of mother love toward her just flood over me. "I am so proud of her! Look at her!" I was shocked. I shook my head. It was so funny.

JIM: You have two grown sons, so mother love is something you knew about.

MILLIE: Mother love is different than any other love. It has its own unique feel. You walk in at night and your child's asleep. It's been one of those heck-of-a days, the kid's been sick, is finally okay and you just have mother feelings. I knew it. I called it right then and there, but I thought it was just funny. I told some people about it, and I told Laura about it. We kind of laughed. I'm not quite old enough to be her mother. I didn't think much more about it. Then, another time, I had the same thing happen. It was just a sweep of mother love—a wave, and I just brushed it off.

Soon, I began to learn about a concept called adoption. I asked, "Where did you get that term? How long has that been around?" The reply was, "Oh, only since biblical times." I began to think about my relationship with Laura in terms of, what kind of bond is it? At one point, I asked Laura, "If you could have any kind of relationship with me you wanted, what would you rather have? Would you rather have me be a friend, a sister, a mother, or what?"

She said, "Oh, soul mate."

I said I could go with that. But, as time went on, I began to realize it was different. God had given me a mother's love for Laura. As I began to understand that, I had some misgivings about how she would receive that. There were so many people who were trying to fix her. I was afraid she would think, here was another person trying to come in and fix her. I had not enough faith that God would prepare her heart, which He did.

I saw some changes in our relationship and thought they were good, and I wanted to talk to her about it. I prepared to ask her if she could pull all the people together inside her—I wanted to tell them something, to see how they would receive it. That was my plan, but it didn't work out that way.

Through a crisis of one of the people inside, God really prompted me to share it with one on the night of a crisis. It was up at a ritualistic site.

JIM: You visited a site where rituals had been practiced?

MILLIE: Yes.

JIM: And that provoked a crisis?

MILLIE: No, the crisis happened and I was taken up there by one of the teen-agers. She was ready for the confrontation—either God was going to do something or she was going to kill herself, and this was the place to do it.

God prompted my heart to tell her He had given me a mother's love for her. It reminded me of a verse where God talks about restoring things that were taken away. At the night of telling, I was surprised how she was able to receive it. For the first time, an angry teen-ager said, "I want to pray," and started in the way she usually started, "Dear God." Because of her background, she had never been able to pray, "Dear Father." So she started, "Dear God," and then she stopped cold. She said, "No. Dear Father."

I talked about God being her father and giving me a mother's love for her. It was a turning point. As I began to share that with the others on the inside, it was received gratefully by everyone. I have a different kind of a mother relationship with each of them, but it's a mother's relationship.

JIM: About how many do you think you are relating to as a mother?

MILLIE: Maybe ten. All have been informed, and I don't know how the others have been affected yet. Since both of us realized God gave me a mother's love for her, it has added a dimension of permanency to the relationship that didn't exist before. There's an uncuttable tie here, even in the term *adoption*—you can disown a natural child but you can't disown an adopted child.

JIM: Do your husband and your adult children now look at her as a member of your family?

MILLIE: My husband, yes. Now that's not to say he is the father, he is "Me Ma's man." She has asked me, "Can he be my dad?" I think these relationships are not something you decide to be, they are something God sort of plants in your awareness. My husband does not see himself as her spiritual father, and so I don't do anything to push that at all. She is scared of him because he is a man. He is wonderful to her. He talks with all her parts. She'll say he's one of only two safe men she knows—you're the other one.

SRA Therapy

JIM: Let's talk about how hard therapy is for ritual abuse survivors.

MILLIE: The dynamics of sexual abuse are incredible to me. To add ritual abuse to that is beyond my comprehension. I don't have anything in my background to relate it to. It is so hard for ritualized parts to relate to anybody. It is isolating simply because so few people can talk about it.

JIM: Once Laura was in a young part, who was telling us about a ritual. She said, "You're not going to believe this! I saw demons coming out of the fire. They went into these people who were hooded, and the people went crazy." I encouraged her to keep telling and she said, "Well, they went into me too! I think they are still there." That is not something you can talk about very easily. Those of us who haven't been there can only try to understand. We know the impact would be absolutely overwhelming.

MILLIE: It's incomprehensible. I remember that session. The things talked about in therapy, we talk about for hours and hours a week.

JIM: You get lots of doses of that kind of memory?

MILLIE: I get doses, I get pictures, and I'm around when things trigger these traumatic memories. Noises, smells, people will trigger all of this, and I mean out of the blue!

JIM: All of a sudden, she will be in a young part, re-experiencing a ritual again?

Denial

MILLIE: Yeah. It's like when you turn a light on and see something too awful. We'll go to the movies, and normally pick a movie that is benign, for obvious reasons, but there may be previews which aren't benign, and I have a cowering child next to me. I can only imagine how devastating it would be to go through that, and not be able to talk about it. That would be a mountain hard to climb. But then, to get there and have them not believe you! There are times she will say, "I don't believe it," and look to see if I believe it because it's so far beyond human comprehension.

JIM: I try to imagine how it would be after a session like that if somebody would be talking about false memories. Has she had anything like that happen, maybe reading an article in the paper which hits her in a part who doesn't know if she can believe her memories?

MILLIE: She saw an afternoon talk show about SRA with somebody who had some questions about it. That other person probably pushed her in the other direction where she said, "No, this is not something to be questioned. It is real." She couldn't bring herself to share how come she knows it is real.

I think the parts of her who haven't experienced the most devastating SRA rituals try to push it away. One of the things they do to push it away is to say, "It can't be real." But, those ones who have been through it have no doubt. There's no waver. There's no confusion about it. The one who experienced it knows it happened.

JIM: What about the ones who have to run her daily life? Do they try not to think about it?

MILLIE: Parts of her try to deny it, but can't, because she's lived it.

JIM: Before you heard her talk about it, had you heard about it?

MILLIE: I'd never heard anything about it, pro or con. Thank God I didn't have to hassle with false memory issues thrown in to confuse anything. I got to see the truth before anybody tried to pollute it.

JIM: Did it ever occur to you she might be making it up?

MILLIE: Never.

JIM: You were there every session! Did it occur to you I might be giving her cues which were helping her see things I wanted her to see?

MILLIE: Absolutely not. I have never seen you give

any kind of cue to her about anything, ever. Not in the beginning with the sexual abuse, not as it went on with SRA. I never saw you feed her one single, solitary line that I thought could be interpreted as a cue, at all.

JIM: You never thought she was making up stories as she went along?

MILLIE: I never thought so at all. No one would willingly put themselves through what she goes through without some kind of impetus driving it. A grown woman doesn't melt onto the lap of another grown woman, as a little child, unless somewhere there was such a need born out of deprivation or cruelty. No. I've never doubted it.

Sometimes she'll say to me, "It's a lie. It's all a lie." I'll say, "Okay." I'm like you, Jim. I don't plant anything. I don't foster anything. I don't try to elaborate on anything she remembers. Then she'll look into my eyes and say, "No, it's not a lie." She wishes it were a lie, and it's not.

Satisfied

JIM: Is there any good coming out of all this hard work?

MILLIE: I can't imagine where she'd be if God hadn't done what He's done in the last four years.

JIM: She was seriously anorexic.

MILLIE: She'd been anorexic, she'd been bulimic, she'd been hospitalized, and she was still in the throes of that eating disorder which could have killed her. That's been gone for three years. She's done a lot of hard, hard work. It's incredible to me how hard people have to work to overcome these things.

JIM: And I believe, sometimes, I may be the cruelest person around to encourage them to do that kind of work, because I have seen how tough it is.

MILLIE: They have to walk through to the other side of it. Otherwise, they're forever in it. We're not done yet. We entered into a process that has no end. Sometimes it's still quite hard, but it's always an adventure with God. God is orchestrating this—He's working in us and through us and around us, teaching us about Himself and about each other! God is at work.

JIM: Let me share something I was reading this morning—Psalm 131. "My heart is not proud, O Lord, my eyes are not haughty; I do not concern myself with great matters or things too wonderful for me." I think that means, "I do not worry about things too incredible for me to understand." King David [the author of the psalm] goes on, "But I have stilled and quieted my soul; like a weaned child with its mother, like a weaned child is my soul within me."

I tried to imagine what it's like to be a weaned child with its mother, and the word *satisfied* seemed to sum it up. Here is King David, who had been through the worst of family circumstances and had struggled with the weight of the whole world on his shoulders as statesman and warrior, but now he's saying, "It's enough for me to be with you, O Lord. I am satisfied."

There is a satisfaction coming to Laura that she wouldn't have gotten without you, Millie. There is a heavenly quality about it that's giving her something she's really needed.

MILLIE: Think of how the mother in Psalm 131 must feel, to have a weaned child. Think of how our Father must feel. Satisfied.

Laura

JIM: You read the conversation I had with Millie last week. What are some of the things you would like to add to that?

Mother's Love

LAURA: One of the things is the adoption, and the realization I didn't have a childhood. I didn't have anything in my life as a child that was normal. And now to be forty years old, to go out and have a play day, I feel like a kid. I go with my mom. To have a mother's love is just so comforting.

JIM: A childhood just isn't a childhood without it.

LAURA: Not everybody gets it. I didn't get it.

JIM: Millie said when you received mother's love from her at a ritual site, it was a turning point for you.

LAURA: When we first met I wanted to be alone. I had built up walls and I didn't want anyone to interfere with my life, including my family. I had set up a system to function that way. When Millie came along, that broke down some walls. I didn't want that and told her so, but it didn't work out that way.

It was slow in the beginning, but flowed very naturally from being gym partners, to friends, then to sisters. So her becoming my mother was just a good next step. It felt right. It wasn't a big, huge change.

JIM: Do you want to say anything about the trip up to the ritual sight, which Millie brought up earlier?

LAURA: It was a turning point for me. I have probably spent most of my life feeling depressed and suicidal. The eating disorder was really about wanting to die, and having a way to die that would not leave my children with the stigma that I had committed suicide. But, I could go to the ritual site, because that was Satan's territory, take a knife and slash my wrists, or do whatever to die. Nothing could stop me because it was on Satan's territory.

Maybe it was a test to see if Millie could stand being on Satan's ground. I was sort of trying to push her away. It's been that way for much of the relationship—I want her to love me, but I push her away. That

night I said, "Give me a reason to not kill myself."
When she started telling me what God had told her
about becoming my mother, it was so overwhelming.
If I killed myself I would be leaving a loving mother
behind. That was not thinkable.

It was a test of God too. I don't think God saved
me from Satan as a child, and was He going to save
me now as an adult? Would God care enough to stop
me? Well, He did!

Jim: It seems He and Millie had been working
together to prepare for that moment. How important
was a mother's love in getting you through the satanic
ritual abuse influence?

Laura: It's kind of hard, because every time I think
about it, Satan says it's not true and it's not from God.
I think it will be a process to learn to say, "Get away,
this is from God."

Programming

Jim: There is a lot of controversy about how many
people have gone through ritual abuse. Some people
say, "Practically nobody" and others say, "Practically
everybody." A lot of people want to know how to overcome the influences. You've been there firsthand. Have
you got some ideas for them?

Laura: Because I was so programmed—I used to
call it brainwashed—how to think and feel and do, and
there are so many triggers, the only way to get out of
it is through God. You can't get out of Satan's work
without God. There is just no other way, and I believe
God provides a way out. I believe that those who go
through SRA without turning to God to help them can
never be deprogrammed.

Jim: If part of the programming is spiritual, power
is available to beat the programming. The Bible says,
"Though we live in the world, we do not wage war as
the world does. The weapons we fight with are not of

the world. On the contrary, they have divine power to demolish strongholds" (2 Cor. 10:3–4). That passage is about beating programming! *Strongholds* means *demonic strongholds*—barricades for demons. Programming produces lies—demonic strongholds which shape people to react in ways contrary to the truth about who they are, and contrary to the truth about who God is. God's power establishes truth to replace deceptive demonic strongholds.

LAURA: They program in such a way that you don't ever talk about it, and you don't remember most of it. You hear of people being hypnotized and waking up not knowing they just acted like a chicken on the stage or something. That's kind of what it's like. You just don't remember at all.

JIM: You were going through life for over thirty years without any conscious recollection that the satanic rituals had even occurred?

LAURA: They started coming to me as flashbacks, not as full memories. I would see strange things with blood, dark and evil, and they just grew and grew. There was one night in particular, I recalled watching a baby who was born and then killed and cut up, and used as a sacrifice. I thought I was just dreaming, but I knew I wasn't. It must have been two or three in the morning. I was so scared I had to call Millie on the phone, and I think a three- or four-year-old called, just talking about this baby. It was so scary. I don't think people get images like that unless they are true.

JIM: How did you get over that?

LAURA: The good thing about dissociation is that you can dissociate! It is a positive thing. You can work with that information a piece at a time. It's taken a lot of therapy; you know that. There are still times I close my eyes and see things I don't want to see, but for the most part, God can take those images away so I don't have to live with them every day. I think you'd go crazy if you had to live with them constantly.

JIM: This has really tested me as a person of faith, to believe that God can work in anything—in everything for our benefit (Rom. 8:28). When I hear about those things happening, I wonder how God can make anything good come out of that.

LAURA: There's a lot we will never know on the face of this earth, but that's how He works. Satan seeks to destroy. God seeks to restore.

There are physical problems I will live with the rest of my life because of the abuse, and sometimes it makes me angry that I will have to suffer for as long as I live. But I accept it, and I'm willing to move on. I don't want to stay stuck in that anger.

JIM: I have heard peoples' thoughts about therapy—what works and what doesn't. I believe people put too much emphasis on therapy and not enough on the home life. Have you got some comments about that?

LAURA: Most of my work was done outside of therapy. After I was hospitalized, I cut myself off from everybody. Things started falling apart. I came to you and said, "I'm dying, Jim. I'm killing myself and I don't know what to do. If you can't help me, that's fine. I'll die." You asked if I would be willing to work for a year and promise not to kill myself.

JIM: It took about four months before I even started to see the dissociation. I was so tuned in to how hurt you were, and you masked the dissociation so well, that I completely missed the diagnosis. The first clue I got was at the beginning of a session one Friday morning at nine o'clock. You said you could see me the next week at the same time on Friday. Then, at the end of that session, I said I'd see you next week at the same time, and you said, "I can't come next Friday at nine." An hour before you said you could come at that time, and now you can't. You are way too bright to not remember our discussion from an hour ago. I didn't see any dissociation, but by the next week I asked you to journal about the different roles you play in life, and we soon found the correct diagnosis. Until the memory slip, I had no idea. It wasn't an obvious diagnosis, by any means.

LAURA: I had a system that functioned very well when it needed to, but I had another system. When it kicked in, I just wanted to die.

JIM: Now let's get back to the question of working on the home life.

LAURA: My home was very chaotic. My husband loves me very much, but doesn't understand how I can be bothered by everyday things. He doesn't understand deep emotional pain. It is very difficult at home. At least I have Millie. Her home is always open, and that's what it took for me to get over the hump. Otherwise, I don't think I ever would have. I needed a mother's love. I needed a soul mate. I needed a sister. I needed all the things Millie became.

JIM: One person finished therapy in about six years, and another went through in about three years. The difference was, one had a therapy partner.

LAURA: I can't imagine that the child parts of me who are afraid of men could have gotten through a session without Millie there. I couldn't tolerate being alone in a room with a man. I wouldn't have stayed in therapy without Millie, when the child parts started having memories. There were times I needed twenty-four-hours-a-day, seven-days-a-week support. I needed it always at my fingertips or I wouldn't have made it. That was a huge commitment on Millie's part. I don't think it has been all fun and games for her. It's been a real sacrifice on her part.

MILLIE: (To Laura) You know what a sacrifice is, don't you? Giving up something good for something better!

More Partners Are Needed

LAURA: One problem I had years ago, was when I had nightmares and could not sleep, seeing horrible pictures all night. If I told my friends they would think I was nuts—a crazy person—and wouldn't have anything to do with me. Especially when the eating disorder was so bad, there were people at church who would ask, "What's your problem? What's going on?" I would say one little thing, and I knew nothing about dissociation at the time, and they'd be gone! It was just too much for them to handle. God had to bring someone as stubborn as Millie into my life to work through this.

JIM: Are you finding people in church are mostly okay now, or does it still seem you cannot open up to them?

LAURA: One-on-one, if it comes up I can be open. I don't walk around announcing, "I have MPD! There's twelve of me today!" If it seems important, I'll discuss it with them. It has to feel safe or I won't.

JIM: I think the frontier still to be explored is to what extent can people really understand and help? I think there are so many people who are not willing to get involved and stick it out like the stubborn Millie! But, that's what it is going to take. There are literally thousands of people who need someone like Millie, but there are not thousands of people ready to be partners. There is a big shortage.

LAURA: I have said all along, "There is a person who needs a Millie."

JIM: Perhaps even more than the right therapist, they need the right partner. If home life isn't encouraging, it doesn't matter if you have the right therapist.

LAURA: Without support, I don't think people get very far. The people where I work are wonderful. They are as much my friends as they are my co-workers. It is a very small office and we get along well, and yet I couldn't tell them these things. I don't know that I ever will. They know I am in therapy and they know it is an issue of abuse, but they know nothing about dissociation. It's like I am afraid to tell them because I'm afraid they will think I'm crazy.

JIM: The whole environment needs to change. We need to view people as adaptive. If people dissociate, it means they have to—it's survival. If they can dissociate, that means they are above average. Not just anybody can operate that way. Dissociation helps in a lot of ways.

LAURA: In the work situation it's wonderful. I have a "work person" who is a perfectionist and a hard worker. I could be as sick as a dog and still show up at work, get into my work person and function beautifully.

JIM: This is the frontier. Some day, when a person says, "I dissociate," people will want to move closer to them and not stay away.

LAURA: Yes, but it is very hard even for people who are trying. They need to be trained. It would be wonderful if people were willing to be trained as partners—partners for life. Hopefully, we will not be in therapy for the rest of our lives (she is such a joker!), but my relationship with Millie will never end. It's neat that God gave me a person who could step in for my family and friends and help me get the things I have missed.

PART III

The Road Ahead

CHAPTER 10:

The psychologists' video conference described in chapter 1 was a scientific step in the right direction. It helped clarify that dissociative identity disorder, formerly called multiple personality disorder, is a known syndrome, and that there is no such thing as false memory syndrome. That term is demeaning to everyone who has recalled painful events—it questions their cries for help and openly challenges everything they say. Instead of leading to help, it is a term which

Getting Help to Those Who Survived Extreme Childhood Abuse

leads to denial. When it is suggested to survivors of abuse that they may have false memory syndrome, this is what they hear: "Please do not tell me anything bad happened." The listener wants to stay in denial, and has no intention of supporting the survivor.

The time has come to employ the scientific knowledge we have. We will keep on learning more about how the mind works, but we know enough at present to help people who have been abused. Instead of endlessly debating FMS, a condition which has not even been defined, let us turn our attention to restoring those who have been abused. When false memory syndrome is attributed to survivors of abuse, their therapeutic progress comes to an abrupt halt, even though science is still waiting for the term to be defined. Let us call off the debate until we get a scientifically sound study which defines false memory syndrome, and points the way to distinguish it from other syndromes. Until then, that term blocks peoples' progress. It contributes only to confusion, not to health.

Dora was on the telephone with a sister, who took it upon herself to speak for the family of origin. "How could you say such a thing about our father? Your psychologist must be giving you false memories."

Dora's recovery is far enough along that she has learned to overcome the blocks set up by false memory accusations. "I'll tell you what doesn't happen in my psychologist's office," Dora replied. "I don't wake up in the middle of the night knowing I've just been raped, trying to wipe all this yucky stuff off my body, and smelling our father."

Dora's explanations led her sister to recognize the truth, and it had nothing to do with false memories. Their father was incestuous. Tears were falling onto both phone receivers for over an hour. "I'm so sorry, Dora, I know you're right. I have kept quiet about this because I was afraid it might be true."

Another family began to recover from the effects of sexual abuse. Recovery involves uncovering the truth, getting some healing, and enjoying the freedom to live in truth. As Dora was telling me about the phone call with her sister, her confidence exuded. She didn't dissociate once. Most of her personalities have blended. She has not cut off contact with members of her family of origin, but things in her family will never be the same. Dora now lives associatively. Family conversations will no longer follow the old rules—"Don't talk, don't think, and don't feel, and protect Daddy." Those rules do not lead to truth—they lead to cover-up.

Dora has forgiven them. The door is now open to family members who can walk in love with Dora on "the road ahead." Walking in love means walking in truth. They go together. Reconciliation means overcoming the effects of incest by all parties, and no longer denying what happened. The road ahead has enough room for everybody, but there is not enough room to bring along unnecessary baggage—denial and cover-up.

Dora's relationships with her husband and children have deepened, and she drinks in life's daily blessings like never before. Her true family, the church friends who have stuck with her through recovery, is her spiritual family. Jesus set the standard for family membership: " 'Who is my mother, and who are my brothers?' Pointing to his disciples, he said, 'Here are my mother and my brothers. For whoever does the will of my Father in heaven is my brother and sister and mother' " (Matt. 12:48–50). Dora has been adopted into her spiritual family, which enjoys walking with her in love and truth. Her family of origin has been invited to join them. Dora hopes that someday, they will all be on that road with her.

"It Couldn't Have Happened to Her"

I met with Chloe's sister for lunch to answer some questions and to hear her concerns about Chloe's therapy. Because the sister had read a false memory article, she had come to believe I created Chloe's condition. The sister's position was simple: If I suggested false memories to Chloe, convinced her they must be true, and am now asking her to live as though those false memories really happened, she will never get better.

"I was with her during our childhood years," she said, "and I can tell you nothing like that happened. Therapy cannot succeed because it is based on something which didn't happen. She will only get worse and worse."

I replied, "If you challenge her about what she remembers, and threaten to sue me, her recovery will stall. You are very important to her, and Chloe says it is extremely painful to have you oppose her. Please believe her and affirm her."

The sister continued, "But I don't remember anything at all like that in her childhood."

"You have not appeared in any of the memories," I answered. "You were not there. It did not happen to you, but her mind tells her terrifying things happened to her. Please support her."

The Opposing Positions

What a dilemma! Roads go in different directions. If people can be convinced that events in their past are true simply because their therapist says so, we are all in trouble. That position will surely take us to the courthouse—and rightly so! If clients are that easily convinced to believe therapists' lies, which end up destroying them and their families, the therapists should be held accountable. If that is true, Chloe's sister will be honor-bound to take me to court.

But sometimes, I wonder. If false memory syndrome proponents really believe minds are that suggestible, why don't they plant some good memories so the troubles will finally come to an end! It would be so simple: "Here's a nice memory for you! I hope you like it. It is better than the one you got from your therapist."

If we think good thoughts, do the bad ones go away? Could good memories be planted in people which would end their struggle with negative feelings? As explained in chapter 2, mind manipulations do not aid people in real life. People either deal with the reality in their life—even if it is grim—or they spend their energy avoiding reality. The position that minds can accept good or bad false memories does not appear strong.

Here is the opposing position. If we find the life-long, disruptive behavior patterns which are often displayed by survivors of abuse,[1] it should be no surprise to find that there are memories of the abusive events which produced the behavior patterns in the first place. The memories need to be uncovered in order for the disruptive behaviors to improve. The problem is the abuse, not the therapy. Somebody other than the therapist belongs in court.

The Bigger Picture

Dr. Freud had great difficulty believing what his clients told him. As they told him their memories of incest, he worked hard to find other ways to interpret their reports. He eventually came to believe their memories were false, and labeled the clients "hysterical neurotics." Do clients profit from having their memories challenged like that? Is a repressed or a dissociated memory hysterical, and nothing more?

These questions need to be answered by the mental health field, not by the legal profession. Lawyers are trained to disbelieve that people tell the truth, and to argue about technical details. Mental health professionals are trained to believe that people benefit when they tell the truth, and trained to explain the hard-to-understand details by looking at the bigger picture.

Here is the bigger picture. When abuse happens, the mind copes in particular ways. Symptoms show. They add up to form a syndrome which points to a history of abuse. Arguing about each symptom is a technical dead end which misses the context—a pattern of symptoms which do not make sense until we look at them as a group, instead of looking at them separately.

Difficult memories can be dealt with. People get better when they honestly assimilate their history. The preceding three chapters document that lives can improve if traumatic memories are dealt with openly. If therapy were based on planting lies in peoples' minds, it would not help them. When disruptive behaviors cease, there is peace. Therapy can help. That is another part of the bigger picture.

As far as I can tell, a very small percentage of therapists still hold on to the position that minds make things up that easily. The vast majority quietly avoid the false memory controversy and stick to their therapy plan, believing that people get better when they deal honestly with their history. To Chloe's sister I say, "Do not take me to court. That will hinder the progress of your loved one. You can help her by believing her."

Accusations Do Not Help

Survivors' progress in therapy is seriously thwarted if accusations against them are not handled mercifully. While therapy is in progress, it is unmerciful to challenge them—they can easily lose their balance and they can lose the progress they have gained. It is better to support them and to trust they will get to the truth about what happened to them.

Here is a Bible verse which has been a guideline and an inspiration for many Christians. "And what does the Lord require of you? To act justly and to love mercy and to walk humbly with your God" (Mic. 6:8). It may at first glance seem impossible to carry out all three requirements. Here is another way to see the verse: Acts of justice and mercy result from walking humbly with God. A humble walk with God is the foundation for justice and mercy; it is the source of the wisdom and power necessary to pursue justice and mercy. As we humbly seek the truth about ourselves, our walk with God will lead us to mercifully seek the restoration of the other party, accused or accuser.

Humility is not easy. We all make mistakes. But, when honest mistakes are pointed out, not all people are repentant. If defensiveness emerges instead of repentance, that is a dubious response. If, as Shakespeare put it, the person "doth protest too much," that indicates a failure to keep emotions under control while the evidence is being considered. All parties suffer from emotionally charged exchanges. Relationships between the accuser and the accused are particularly vulnerable. Care should be taken to avoid volatile accusations against either party.

Controlling emotions about this topic is an art which many people have yet to refine. Rampant emotions often seem to be the rule instead of the exception. It is clear, however, that nobody is helped by staying intense about false memory syndrome-related issues. All parties need to stay calm as issues unfold. In cases where emotional lids do not stay on, there is a marked danger of irreparably harming relationships.

Here is an example taken from someone mentioned in my first book, of telling the truth about abuse in a clear, yet helpful way. As Beth's therapy approached its completion, she wrote a letter to her father, a convicted sex offender. It was brief and did not attempt to set the record straight about his abuse. She told him his life has been miserable, and he needs the Lord. She went on to say if he continues to go his own way he will die a miserable man. She invited him to follow Christ in order to receive the healing which had eluded him his whole life. He did not write a return letter, and as far as I know, their relationship has remained distant. He may die a miserable man, but not because his daughter accused him. His misery has been his own creation, and he did not accept Beth's invitation to seek health.

Denial Leads to Cover-Up

If between forty and eighty million United States citizens have been abused, can we afford to give them all public assistance for their physical and psychological recovery? No mental health system is ready for that, and no government can afford to pay professionals for the countless hours that millions of abuse survivors will need for recovery. Politicians and mental health leaders have no alternative but to deny the problem is that large. If abuse is, in fact, that extensive, the problem will eventually be too large to deny. At that point, the health care delivery system will either undergo some changes or denial will increase. If increased denial does not work, cover-up will necessarily replace honest assessment of the problem.

We are in danger of becoming a citizenry without a properly organized way to deal with the magnitude of the child abuse problem. Some professionals believe we have already reached that point. Desperate people have telephoned me to see if I know any therapists in their city. They have looked everywhere they can think of and report a tremendous lack of resources for trauma recovery. For them, the system is already failing.

Resources

Community

An old African saying goes like this: "It takes a whole village to raise a child." That truth applies to people in therapy. It takes more than a therapist and more than a loving family to restore people who have been hurt in childhood. It takes a whole community of people who can be available at a moment's notice. The village needs to be ready to protect them and to encourage their growth.

Survivors of abuse cannot be expected to improve in a climate where their feelings are minimized and where accusations intimidate them. They try to keep going without therapy, but it is hard to deal with the powerful feelings which come up. Because of the authoritative way false memory presentations are delivered, survivors of abuse often choose to suffer in silence—avoid their powerful feelings—rather than face minimization and accusation.

They should be encouraged to deal honestly and openly with their life issues. Getting help to those who have survived extreme childhood abuse means supporting them while they are dealing with powerful feelings. Their village needs to encourage survivors to get through any memories and any conflicts which stand between them and a better life.

The tremendous need for understanding by those who surround survivors in their everyday life has shaped this book. The language and concepts have been chosen to increase knowledge in communities. People in many walks of life can encourage, appreciate, and support those whose lives have been interrupted by childhood abuse.

Survivors need a community which will encourage them to contribute to the community. Living a healthy life means receiving from the community and giving something back. Dissociation preserves natural talents by keeping them walled off from strong feelings. Survivors who dissociate, routinely have abundant talents. The community's task is to affirm those talents and to encourage the survivor to use them for the benefit of the whole community.

Part II illustrates how an enriching community can bring about restoration. Further evidence of this comes from a survey I conducted last year. To find out what lessons churches are learning, I got on the phone and found over forty churches with programs for survivors of abuse around the country. Twenty-four leaders in those churches returned questionnaires, and here are some pertinent findings:

1. When churches minister to dissociators, without bringing them into the mainstream of the church as those who minister, church resources tend to get depleted. A ministry directed to helping survivors does not tend to work. They need to be incorporated into the mainstream of church life on ministry teams, prayer teams, or wherever they can express their natural talents. They do best as members of ongoing groups which have nothing to do with therapy, like choir, Sunday school, or Bible study groups. Prayer groups, praise and worship programs, or "problems-in-living" groups which include spouses and therapy partners, are especially helpful. Giving life to them and receiving life from them must be a two-way street. Resources are to be shared and everyone benefits.

2. Lay persons can carry out effective programs for a very low cost to the church, usually with professionals in an advisory capacity. Many of the small churches in the survey have designated about one thousand dollars per year to subsidize therapy costs. Getting help to survivors of abuse does not have to drain the national budget. They can receive help and we can afford to give them help in communities which consider that a priority. Here is one response to my survey which highlights the power of such programs:

> To have a church that is supportive for this kind of healing seems tantamount to healing. Many of these women have come from community churches which have not understood, and have felt spiritually abused by their pastors and church leaders. Knowing they can sit in the pews on Sunday morning without feeling condemned by the sermon is of great encouragement for them. Our church is the only one in our area which so

far has ventured to reach out to hurting people in this way. One of the women who has attended this group for three years has driven seventy-five miles one way every week. There are now some other local churches making plans to begin groups, and this is exciting to hear about! The need is so great! I am so excited to see all that God has unfolded right before my very own eyes! I have seen many miracles happen and it is only the beginning.

3. If the senior pastor knows a dissociator personally, the program has a good chance of gaining acceptance. Otherwise, it tends to remain on the periphery of church life. It is important to get the senior pastor's attention and support before starting this kind of a program, because support is needed at the highest level of authority.

4. Church leaders in these programs need to network with leaders of similar programs in other churches. Questions and problems will come up which require sharing and support. There is a lot to learn, and leaders dedicated to working in this area will benefit from open lines of communication with fellow workers.

5. Training sessions for church leaders about dissociation and trauma recovery have been important. Many ideas are new, so time needs to be set aside for training.[2]

6. Church leaders who work with abuse survivors believe ritual abuse accounts are real. In these cases clients are free to open up about memories without fear of being unfairly confronted. On twenty-three out of twenty-four questionnaires, program leaders thoughtfully reflected that the ritual accounts seem true, and one respondent left that question blank. This finding is not different from a survey already discussed, where therapists were found to believe ritual accounts are

true by a margin of twenty-two to one (see chapter 6). Therapists and church leaders who have experience in working with ritual abuse survivors believe them, and this fact needs to be emphasized: Highly trained, professional people who have spent hundreds of hours with survivors of ritual abuse are convinced they are telling the truth. Here are some leaders' responses.

• We assume the reality of the memory and deal with it as such. We do not deny it without cause. We do not confront unless there is significant contrary evidence.

• I tend to believe them based on the detail of descriptions, the dynamics and affect surrounding the reporting, the consistency within the system/person over time, and the similarities between the reports of different people without any common source.

• Eighty-five percent is accurate, but some fantasy material gets mixed in. [This is consistent with the model in chapter 2 about distortions.]

• Most of the time actual events are reported. However, one person's false memories turned out to be a [wounded] child personality. When that was taken care of, life became more mature.

Families and Friends

Establishing a maturing self requires intimacy. To be fully human is to love and to live in loving relationships. Raising a child means bestowing love on the child and having the child learn to give love in return. The community contributes to the life and health of families, but it must be the families and close friends who impart the knowledge of how to live a life of love.

Where love cannot be counted on during childhood, people are not properly trained to give and receive love, nor to protect the self during adulthood. Vulnerable and lacking self-confidence, they need to learn to give and receive love more effectively and to improve their skills in protecting the self. While those skills are being developed, families and friends are to provide extra love and extra protection. Dr. Henry Cloud and Dr. John Townsend put it this way: "Don't even try to start setting limits [protecting the self] until you have entered into deep, abiding attachments with people who will love you no matter what. Our deepest need is to belong, to be in a relationship, to have a spiritual and emotional 'home.' "[3]

Family members and friends of abused persons will come in contact with pain. Weakness and inner conflicts will be exposed and challenged, but everything can be viewed as a chance to grow. If friends welcome growth and change, the survivor is encouraged to do likewise, but supportive friends can sometimes cautiously step away from difficulties which come up. A word of encouragement seems appropriate:

> You are the friend of someone who has been abused, and you are untrained, inexperienced, and scared. If I am accurate so far, then you have also seriously thought about backing out of the relationship with your abused friend.
>
> My counsel to you is simple: Don't back off from the frightening terrain of a wounded heart. You may say the wrong things and even cause more harm, but the worst harm is to turn your back. Accept your limitations, but also acknowledge the fact that you are on the front lines of the battle. You may not like to hear it, but the fact is, you are a foot soldier, an infantryman who is often the first to take the fire of the enemy. As a therapist, I see your friend once, or maybe twice a week. You see her every day. I deal with significant issues in her soul, but you talk about the same issues and even more. I may be necessary to the process, but you are even more so. Let me say it again. You are very

important as a friend who will pray, talk, laugh, cry, read, embrace, shout, bake cookies, drive to Little League, and live life in intimate proximity. Don't allow your inexperience or your own personal past to keep you from loving well.[4]

Therapy Partners

People who volunteer for a position as a therapy partner usually do not carry out their responsibilities very well. What a paradox! On the one hand, I say the need for caring therapy partners is immense, but yet, I discourage prospective partners from volunteering.

The most effective therapy partners are people already in relationships with the client before therapy began. Most of these partners were already positively involved, and just needed some coaching to deliver their love more openly. Robert, William, and Millie are stellar examples, whose contributions are highlighted in Part II. They were available as therapy began and their relationships with the survivors grew.

It looks like people willing to be therapy partners are advised to deepen relationships with people they already know. As Millie once put it, "I'm not helping Laura. I'm just living honestly with her. If help comes out of that, I am very happy." If you have friends who are survivors of abuse, please live honestly with them. Pray with them, take their kids to Little League, and let your relationship grow. It is a challenge to share their suffering. If you are led to become a therapy partner, you are the lucky one. You have been granted a privileged place—alongside your friend on the road ahead.

Therapists

The resources footnoted in Part I will help therapists refine their therapeutic interventions. This chapter may assist therapists in creating a realistic role in the future's health care delivery system:

• Trauma recovery will comprise a larger percent of the caseloads. Victims of many kinds of abuse, and abuse perpetrators, will look for care. Continuing education will be needed to help therapists keep up in this fast-moving field. Consultation and support teams will also play an important role in keeping up.

• Funds will shrink. Public funding will be insufficient, so private funding will be needed. Those who have survived extreme abuse often require two to five hours of therapy per week. Input from communities is vital for funding and for assisting in the therapeutic work itself. Volunteers may provide help with problems in living, which will allow therapists to focus on internal work and reduce the number of paid hours.

• The primary arena for help will be the client's living environment, rather than the therapist's office. Therapists are not usually the ones who can deliver enough love to carry a person through crises. Trauma recovery requires developing deep and lasting friendships, and living in a caring community. That is where crises will be overcome, which means therapists will be involved regularly with key people in clients' lives. Therapists will need to find ways to work with clients' families and communities.

• Therapists will need to encourage clients to open up about spiritual issues. So far, the clinical community wants to define itself apart from the spiritual community. That does not work for people who consider themselves spiritual beings. This may be problematic for some time, since the attitude about keeping spiritual issues separate from psychological issues is deeply entrenched. However, it seems important to challenge that attitude in the case of trauma survivors: They have been subjected to authorities who tell them exactly what they can and cannot talk about. It makes more sense to help them see therapists as authorities who encourage clients to talk about whatever is needed. It is not therapeutic to prohibit discussions about the spiritual dimension of life, so many therapists will need to learn new approaches to spirituality.

Spiritual Resources

A community and a family which share the client's spiritual perspective are important resources. The therapist's spiritual world needs to be compatible with the client's spiritual world in order to be a spiritual resource. To be allowed to deal with spiritual issues is vital, especially if there is spiritual or religious abuse in the client's background.

A question debated by therapists is whether it is ethical to bring up spiritual issues during therapy. I believe psychology is moving in the right direction concerning that question. The *DSM-IV* includes a category among "Other Conditions That May be a Focus of Clinical Attention," which paves the way for the proper handling of spiritual material.[5] The category reads like this:

> Religious or Spiritual Problem. This category can be used when the focus of clinical attention is a religious or spiritual problem. Examples include distressing experiences that involve loss or questioning of faith, problems associated with conversion to a new faith, or questioning of spiritual values that may not necessarily be related to an organized church or religious institution. (page 685)

In my first months as a psychology intern in a non-Christian clinic, I found that people routinely seek therapists who are spiritually compatible. The woman at the switchboard would route calls to me when a prospective client wanted to receive therapy from a Christian. Everybody on staff knew that Christian clients were supposed to be lined up with Christian therapists. My supervisor told me it was perfectly okay to pray with clients, but I should probably not include the fact that we prayed in the official case notes. Public funding was involved, and the administration did not want to jeopardize their public position, but yet, found it important to let people pray if they so desired. I expect that kind of implicit approval of handling spiritual issues has continued, and has led therapists to include the category for religious and spiritual problems in the *DSM-IV*.

Mental health and spiritual health are intertwined. My clients keep on giving me examples. In her journal, Alexi wrote about the role of spiritual issues in her recovery, and has given me permission to use some of it here.

> As a trauma survivor, I know there is no violation that ravages the human spirit as does ritual abuse. Some psychologists urge therapists to avoid the spiritual dimension of healing, as if that were in the client's best interest, but as a religious person, I regard spiritual restoration as highly as I do the psychological aspect. My total recovery is not only enhanced, but accelerated by processing spiritual issues. Ritual abuse survivors must explore the many distortions of their spirituality, because it always impacts spiritual perceptions. As a Christian, I need to seek answers for the toughest spiritual questions, and to clear up distortions about love, trust, security, and about God and His Word.

> When I used to read from the Old Testament, I comprehended only the suffering of the Israelites. This year is different. I can finally see God's overwhelming love for His people. God actively endeavored to protect, heal, and restore them, just as He's done with me.

> From the very first evil choice a perpetrator made

to defile me, God embraced me. Then He handed me every defense, every tool and coping skill, every person and facility I needed to protect, heal, and restore my true nature. God facilitates preservation. There is a Bible passage in Paul's first letter to the Corinthians (chapter 10, verse 13) which promises a way of escape for every trial life delivers. For those who suffer at the hands of strangers, friends, and even family, there are both natural and supernatural escape routes, leading to self-preservation.

The first escape route God supplied for me was dissociation. The "amnesic anesthetic" protected me from the reality of severe trauma. There are other ways God intervenes. I envy children like Isaac in the Old Testament. God's hand literally reached down and stopped the knife from destroying him. I hear accounts by survivors whose perpetrators were stopped mid-stream in abusive acts. Other children were not spared from the knife. It is reassuring to me that God escorts some children away from sadistic hands, and heals them all at once in heaven.

God's grace, my diligence, and the faithful help of my support system are paying off. Finally, I can marvel at the intricacies of my own custom-made plan for preservation, which my heavenly Father carried me through from day one.

I can now savor the insight into God's character that I am gaining through spiritual recovery. God lavishes upon survivors His strength, a supernatural ability to love, and somehow, a way to forgive. He hands us tools reserved for those who travel the deepest valleys.

Jesus knew that twenty years ago, an innocent little girl would need His intervention to survive.

He never left me. Thank God for the gift of dissociation, and thank God for guiding me through the harsh realities of abuse.

The "Road Ahead" will encourage wholeness. Psychological, spiritual, and medical resources will complement each other along the way. Tears fill my eyes as I look forward to a time when recovery from abuse will be encouraged by the whole community. It is such a struggle for survivors without resources, and it does not have to be that way.

APPENDIX A:

Victims usually react to ritual abuse by dissociating. This form of abuse has received little documentation, but Cavalcade Productions [7360 Potter Valley Rd, Ukiah, CA 95482; call (800) 345-5530, or (707) 743-1168 in California] has good RA documentary and educational videos. Their introductory videos, "Children at Risk: Ritual Abuse in America" and "True/Not True: When Memories Can Be Trusted," are highly recommended.

Successful Ritual Abuse Prosecutions

Cavalcade Productions provided the following list of successful ritual abuse prosecutions. In most cases the ritual aspect was not introduced in court, but was clearly indicated by the accounts of the victims.

1984. Niles, Michigan: The husband of a day-care operator was convicted. Miami, Florida: A couple went to prison because of abuses at the Country Walk day-care. Malden, Massachusetts: The Fells Acre day-care case resulted in guilty verdicts.

1987. Roseburg, Oregon: Three Gallup day-care facilities were the scene of crimes which resulted in the conviction of a minister, his wife, and his son. Lehi, Utah: A man was convicted of abusing his own children. Many other adults were identified as perpetrators of satanic ritual abuse.

1988. Carson City, Nevada: A woman and her nephew were convicted of criminal acts against children in a baby-sitting service. Maplewood, New Jersey: A woman was convicted of offenses at the Wee Care Daycare. Santa Rosa, California: A man and a woman plea bargained, and received prison terms. The prosecutor mentioned ritual aspects of the crimes, and child victims described satanic rituals.

1989. Stuart, Florida: A man pleaded guilty to charges of abuse at the Montessori school where he was principal. His secretary was also found guilty.

1990. Akron, Colorado: Two men pled guilty to molesting children at the day-care operated by their grandmother, who received a lesser sentence. A *Denver Post* story on the case included ritual allegations by a child victim.

1992. Mansfield, Ohio: Two teen-age baby sitters at a church were sent to prison for abusing children during church functions. Children reported witnessing ritual acts. Edenton, North Carolina: The owner of the Little Rascals Day Care Center, was found guilty of ninety-nine counts of sexual abuse. Twelve children testified in court, and one described how the perpetrators would pray, "Oh devil, destroy these children." Johnston County, North Carolina: A man was convicted on three counts of sexual acts and was given three consecutive life sentences for abusing children at a baby-sitting facility. Children described capes, candles, robes, and video cameras. Austin, Texas: Two people were convicted of aggravated sexual assault on a child who attended Fran's Daycare. Accounts of ritual abuse have been related by the children.

The first section determines if the person can dissociate, the second indicates if dissociation is observable, and the third shows if there is a history

Dissociative Indicators Scale

of dissociative behavior patterns. These may be present separately or jointly in at least one personality state.

Personality Characteristics

__ 1. High intelligence.

__ 2. High creativity—music, writing, drama, or art, for example.

__ 3. High suggestibility/ability to use imagery.

__ 4. Urgency about time—a rush to get finished with therapy or a general urgency about life.

__ 5. A sense of extreme deprivation—feeling they have been "ripped off" most of their life.

__ 6. Inappropriate need to please—a need to be acceptable to everyone.
(four or more suggests Dissociative Identity Disorder)

Clinical Observables

__ 7. Secretiveness or refusal to reveal personal experiences.

__ 8. *Amnesia for previously covered material.

__ 9. *Headaches or dizziness of sudden onset during therapy.

___ 10. *Evidence of internal dialog.
___ 11. Sudden shift in mood or voice.
___ 12. *Flashback—reliving a traumatic experience.
      (four or more suggests DID)

Outside Data

___ 13. Uneven achievement in school.
___ 14. *Reports of hearing inner voices.
___ 15. *History of sleep disturbances.
___ 16. *Difficulty finding their parked car.
___ 17. *Inordinate indecision about which clothes to wear.
___ 18. Denial of actions that were clearly observed by others.
      (four or more suggests DID)
      *Scores on starred items strongly suggest DID.

Notes

Chapter 1

1. Craig Lockwood is a journalist who has done a good job of chronicling how the press has handled the ritual abuse controversy in *Other Altars: Roots and Realities of Cultic and Satanic Ritual Abuse and Multiple Personality Disorder* (Minneapolis: Compcare Publishers, 1993). It strongly supports the notion that those who have reported ritual abuse are credible witnesses.

2. This is the first case discussed by Lenore Terr, M.D., in *Unchained Memories: True Stories of Traumatic Memories, Lost and Found* (New York: BasicBooks, 1994). Dr. Terr's respect for those who have suffered, and her dogged determination to seek the truth, make this a book that must be read.

3. A Nation's Shame: Fatal Child Abuse and Neglect in the United States, A Report of the U.S. Advisory Board on Child Abuse and Neglect. April 1995, 9.

4. Gloria and her husband, William, share their views in chapter 8: "Making a Difference."

5. "The American Psychological Association Monitor," vol. 26, no. 4 (April 1995).

6. Untitled manuscript about recovering from extreme abuse, including ritual abuse.

Chapter 2

1. A doctoral dissertation concluded that an assessment tool listed in my first book, *Uncovering the Mystery of*

MPD, is accurate. (Eugene Van Dusseldorp, "The Validity of the Dissociative Indicators Scale for Assessing Dissociative Identity Disorder," *Dissertation Abstracts,* 1995.) Items on that scale, often suggest MPD/DID. For details see chapter 4 of *Uncovering the Mystery of MPD.* The power of this tool is that it provides more information than a "symptoms checklist."

2. My second book, *More than Survivors: Conversations with Multiple Personality Clients* (Nashville: Thomas Nelson, 1992) illustrates that these are splendid people, much maligned by misguided publicity.

3. About 97% of those with MPD have been abused during early childhood, according to researchers. In over 80% of the cases the abuse was sexual.

4. Recent articles have shed light on how dissociation is different from repression. These two articles contribute to the body of literature about that subject.

Bessel A. van der Kolk, M.D., "The Body Keeps the Score: Memory and the Evolving Psychobiology of Post-traumatic Stress" (Boston, MA: Harvard Medical School, 1994).

Jody Messler Davies, Ph.D., and Mary Gail Frawley, Ph.D., "Treating the Adult Survivor of Childhood Sexual Abuse" (New York: Harper Collins, 1994).

5. The "Dissociative Indicators Scale" (see note 1, chapter 2) looks for dissociative behavior patterns, past and present. Another widely used assessment tool for dissociative conditions is the "Structured Clinical Interview for DSM-IV Dissociative Disorders" (Marlene Steinberg, M.D., Washington, DC: American Psychiatric Press, Inc., 1993). It also checks for dissociative patterns, both past and present, in its assessment procedures.

Chapter 3

1. In-depth accounts from nine cases are found in *More than Survivors: Conversations with Multiple Personality*

Clients, James G. Friesen, (Nashville, TN: Thomas Nelson, 1992). Contributions from many survivors are included in *Multiple Personality from the Inside Out* (Lutherville, MD: Sidran Press, 1991).

Chapter 4

1. Call Cavalcade Productions at (800) 345-5530 or in California, (707) 743-1168, or write to them at 7360 Potter Valley Rd., Ukiah, CA 95482.

2. James G. Friesen, *More than Survivors: Conversations with Multiple Personality Clients* (Nashville, TN: Thomas Nelson, 1992).

3. Ralph Allison, *Minds in Many Pieces* (New York: Rawson-Wade, 1980).

4. International Society for the Study of Dissociation. 5700 Old Orchard Rd., First Floor, Skokie, IL 60077-1057.

5. At present the organization headquarters is located in Dallas, Texas. For further information call (817) 354-1389.

6. To learn about these books, call the Sidran Foundation at (410) 825-8888. They mail annotated bibliographies which describe over sixty books on MPD/DID, and include an order form to purchase any of the books.

Chapter 5

1. My first book, *Uncovering the Mystery of MPD*, documents this more fully in chapter 3: "Satanic Ritual Abuse." A multidisciplinary source is The Society for the Investigation, Treatment and Prevention of Ritual and Cult Abuse, P.O. Box 835564, Richardson, TX 75083-5564.

2. "Ritual Abuse: Definitions, Glossary, the Use of Mind Control." Report of the Ritual Abuse Task Force, Los Angeles County Commission for Women, 1 September 1994. This thirty-six page book includes references for further reading, names and addresses of newsletters, journals, videotapes, audiotapes, organizations, and

hotlines. Write to 383 Hall of Administration, 500 W. Temple, Los Angeles, CA 90012, or call (213) 974-1455.

3. Dale McCulley, "Satanic Ritual Abuse: A Question of Memory," *Journal of Psychology and Theology,* vol. 22, no. 3, 167-172.

Chapter 6

1. A survey of therapists in San Diego county found 30% of the responding therapists reported they are working with RA survivors—over 130 therapists in one county! The number of people with RA memories in San Diego county could very easily be over five hundred, considering that many therapists are seeing more than one such case, and other survivors are not in therapy. I know of only one case that has gone to court in that county, while the other people have remained out of the public spotlight. The survey is on file at the Los Angeles County Commission for Women, Ritual Abuse Task Force. (213) 974-1455.

2. "Therapists' Experiences of the Effects of Working with Dissociative Patients" by Nancy E. Perry, Ph.D., Milwaukee, Wisconsin. I received a six-page report about the results because I participated in the study, but do not know if the results have been officially published.

3. James A. Chu, M.D., "Ten Traps for Therapists in the Treatment of Trauma Survivors," *Dissociation,* vol. 1, no. 4 (December 1988).

4. Some estimates are higher but there are few conclusive studies. For further data call the National Coalition Against Pornography: (513) 521-6227. Another resource is D. Mitchell Whitman's book: *Child Sexual Abuse: A Teaching Manual for Clergy and Other Christian Leaders* (P.O. Box 1456, Bellingham, WA, 98227).

Chapter 8

1. "Job" is the 18th book in the Old Testament. This quote is taken from Job, chapter 42.

2. Components of dissociation are discussed in *Uncovering the Mystery of MPD,* page 114. Components can come into awareness separately. The mind sees pictures of what happened, which is one component. Feelings are remembered, and that component is stored in a different part of the brain. There is also a body component. Those sensations are recorded in the brain's sensory-motor area, and nothing distorts what the body remembers. It does not lie. If a body remembers being abused, we know there was abuse.

Chapter 9

1. Tom and Linda have found that incorporation of their "bio-psycho-socio-theological framework" has substantially reduced hospitalization for dissociative clients. Please direct questions concerning their cognitive-behavioral work with dissociative and addictive clients to Brownback, Mason and Associates in Allentown, Pennsylvania.

Chapter 10

1. Dr. Lenore Terr does a nice job of explaining how trauma-specific symptoms confirm the gist of a memory, and how lifelong behavior patterns result. See *Unchained Memories: True Stories of Traumatic Memories, Lost and Found* (New York: BasicBooks, 1994).

2. *Care-Giving: The Cornerstone of Healing* by Cheryl Knight and Jo Getzinger, (317) 455-1116, is directed to those who are part of such a church program. C.A.R.E., Inc., the organization which produced this book, also conducts trauma recovery training seminars in churches.

3. Henry Cloud and John Townsend, *Boundaries* (Grand Rapids, Michigan: Zondervan Publishing House, 1992), 64.

4. Dan Allender, *The Wounded Heart* (Colorado Springs: NavPress, 1990).

5. See page 9 for a discussion of the *Diagnostic and Statistical Manual of Mental Disorders,* Fourth Edition (1994).

We welcome comments from our readers. Feel free
to write to us at the following address:

Editorial Department
Huntington House Publishers
P.O. Box 53788
Lafayette, LA 70505

===

More Good Books from
Huntington House

A Jewish Conservative
Looks at Pagan America
by Don Feder

With eloquence and insight that rival essayists of antiquity,
Don Feder's pen finds his targets in the enemies of God,
family, and American tradition and morality. Deftly . . .
delightfully . . . the master allegorist and Titian with a
typewriter brings clarity to the most complex sociological
issues and invokes giggles and wry smiles from both
followers and foes. Feder is Jewish to the core, and he finds
in his Judaism no inconsistency with an American Judeo-
Christian ethic. Questions of morality plague school
administrators, district court judges, senators,
congressmen, parents, and employers; they are wrestling
for answers in a "changing world." Feder challenges this
generation and directs inquirers to the original books of
wisdom: the Torah and the Bible.

ISBN 1-56384-036-7 Trade Paper
ISBN 1-56384-037-5 Hardcover

Getting Out:
An Escape Manual for Abused Women
by Kathy L. Cawthon

Four million women are physically assaulted by their husbands, ex-husbands, and boyfriends each year. Of these millions of women, nearly 4,000 die. Kathy Cawthon, herself a former victim of abuse, uses her own experience and the expertise of law enforcement personnel to guide the reader through the process of escaping an abusive relationship. *Getting Out* also shows readers how they can become whole and healthy individuals instead of victims, giving them hope for a better life in the future.

ISBN 1-56384-093-6

I Shot an Elephant in My Pajamas—
The Morrie Ryskind Story
by Morrie Ryskind with John H. M. Roberts

The Morrie Ryskind story is a classic American success story. The son of Russian Jewish immigrants, Ryskind went on to attend Columbia University and achieve legendary fame on Broadway and in Hollywood, win the Pulitzer Prize, and become a noted nationally syndicated columnist. Writing with his legendary theatrical collaborators George S. Kaufman and George and Ira Gershwin, their political satires had an enormous impact on the development of the musical comedy. In Hollywood, many classic films and four of the Marx Brothers' sublime romps also bear the signatory stamp of genius—Morrie Ryskind. Forced by his increasingly conservative views to abandon script-writing in Hollywood, Ryskind had the satisfaction near the end of his life to welcome into his home his old friend, the newly elected President of the United States, Ronald Reagan.

ISBN 1-56384-000-6

Political Correctness:
The Cloning of the American Mind
by David Thibodaux, Ph.D.

The author, a professor of literature at the University of Southwestern Louisiana, confronts head on the movement that is now being called Political Correctness. Political correctness, says Thibodaux, "is an umbrella under which advocates of civil rights, gay and lesbian rights, feminism, and environmental causes have gathered." To incur the wrath of these groups, one only has to disagree with them on political, moral, or social issues. To express traditionally Western concepts in universities today can result in not only ostracism, but even suspension. (According to a recent "McNeil-Lehrer News Hour" report, one student was suspended for discussing the reality of the moral law with an avowed homosexual. He was reinstated only after he apologized.)

ISBN 1-56384-026-X

Beyond Political Correctness:
Are There Limits to This Lunacy?
by David Thibodaux

Author of the best-selling *Political Correctness: The Cloning of the American Mind,* Dr. David Thibodaux now presents his long awaited sequel—*Beyond Political Correctness: Are There Limits to This Lunacy?* The politically correct movement has now moved beyond college campuses. The movement has succeeded in turning the educational system of this country into a system of indoctrination. Its effect on education was predictable: steadily declining scores on every conceivable test which measures student performance; and, increasing numbers of college freshmen who know a great deal about condoms, homosexuality, and abortion, but whose basic skills in language, math, and science are alarmingly deficient.

ISBN 1-56384-066-9

Out of Control—
Who's Watching Our Child
Protection Agencies?

by Brenda Scott

This book of horror stories is true. The deplorable and unauthorized might of Child Protection Services is capable of reaching into and destroying any home in America. No matter how innocent and happy your family may be, you are one accusation away from disaster. Social workers are allowed to violate constitutional rights and often become judge, jury, and executioner. Innocent parents may appear on computer registers and be branded "child abuser" for life. Every year, it is estimated that over 1 million people are falsely accused of child abuse in this country. You could be next, says author and speaker Brenda Scott.

ISBN 1-56384-069-3

Journey into Darkness: Nowhere to Land

by Stephen L. Arrington

This story begins on Hawaii's glistening sands and ends in the mysterious deep with the Great White Shark. In between, he found himself trapped in the drug smuggling trade—unwittingly becoming the "Fall Guy" in the highly publicized John Z. DeLorean drug case. Naval career shattered, his youthful innocence tested, and friends and family put to the test of loyalty, Arrington locked on one truth during his savage stay in prison and endeavors to share that critical truth now. Focusing on a single important message to young people—to stay away from drugs—the author recounts his horrifying prison experience and allows the reader to take a peek at the source of hope and courage that helped him survive.

ISBN 1-56384-003-3

The Walking Wounded
A Look at Faith Theology
by Jeremy Reynalds

Is the faith movement saving souls—or destroying lives? After a pastor's wife dies of cancer, he is told that it was due to a lack of faith. A woman in Sweden is so traumatized by the faith movement that she enters a treatment program for ex-cult members to recover. According to a recent study cited by the author, many former faith members appear to have developed severe psychiatric problems from their experiences. Read what he has to say and decide for yourself whether word of faith doctrine is orthodox Christianity or outright heresy.

ISBN 1-56384-076-6

Kinsey, Sex and Fraud:
The Indoctrination of a People
by Dr. Judith A. Reisman and Edward Eichel

Kinsey, Sex and Fraud describes the research of Alfred Kinsey which shaped Western society's beliefs and understanding of the nature of human sexuality. His unchallenged conclusions are taught at every level of education—elementary, high school, and college—and quoted in textbooks as undisputed truth. The authors clearly demonstrate that Kinsey's research involved illegal experimentations on several hundred children. The survey was carried out on a non-representative group of Americans, including disproportionately large numbers of sex offenders, prostitutes, prison inmates, and exhibitionists.

ISBN 0-910311-20-X

ORDER THESE HUNTINGTON HOUSE BOOKS

*Available in Salt Series

Available at bookstores everywhere or order direct from:
Huntington House Publishers • P.O. Box 53788 • Lafayette, LA 70505
Send check/money order. For faster service use VISA/MASTERCARD.
Call toll-free 1-800-749-4009.
Add: Freight and handling, $3.50 for the first book ordered, and $.50 for
each additional book up to 5 books.